IN-A-FLASH

MATH

THOMSON
PETERSON'S

Australia • Canada • Mexico • Singapore • Spain • United Kingdom • United States

About The Thomson Corporation and Peterson's

With revenues approaching US$6 billion, The Thomson Corporation (www.thomson.com) is a leading global provider of integrated information solutions for business, education, and professional customers. Its Learning businesses and brands (www.thomsonlearning.com) serve the needs of individuals, learning institutions, and corporations with products and services for both traditional and distributed learning.

Peterson's, part of The Thomson Corporation, is one of the nation's most respected providers of lifelong learning online resources, software, reference guides, and books. The Education Supersite^{SM} at www.petersons.com—the Internet's most heavily traveled education resource—has searchable databases and interactive tools for contacting U.S.-accredited institutions and programs. In addition, Peterson's serves more than 105 million education consumers annually.

CONTENTS

About In-A-Flash Math 1
How to Use In-A-Flash Math 1

Strategies that Really Work 4
Focus on What's Actually Being Asked 1
When in Doubt, Try Something 1
Round Off and "Guesstimate" Freely 5
If Stymied, Plug in an Answer and Work Backward 7

SAT Math Test 19

Solutions to Grid-In Problems 85

ACT Assessment Math Test 87

Concept-to-Problem Index 161

ABOUT IN-A-FLASH: MATH

In-A-Flash: Math is your private tutor. Instead of trying to cram more arithmetic, algebra, and geometry lessons onto thinner paper, with smaller type, *In-A-Flash: Math* recreates a math SAT and a math ACT Assessment and walks you through them. If you have difficulty with a question, you can read the detailed answer that follows on the next page. When you understand a problem, you can check the answer quickly and instead focus on areas where you need to study.

To write *In-A-Flash: Math* we analyzed one SAT exam and one ACT Assessment exam. For each problem on the real tests, we wrote a new problem that tests the same skills at the same difficulty level and placed it in our test in the same position as we found it on the exams. This guarantees that what you're working with here models what you'll see when you sit down to take the "real thing." The structure is the same; the skills tested are the same; the difficulty of the problems is the same; and the types of problems are the same.

We then wrote detailed answers to each of the 120 problems, describing explicitly the math skill that each question tests. On page 141 we provide a *Concept-to-Problem* index. If after reviewing a problem solution you decide that you need more practice with a particular math skill, you can individualize your study plan and save time by looking the skill up in the index and focusing on those problems that exercise the skill.

How to Use *In-A-Flash: Math*
Dig right in! The best practice is to do math problems. As you're doing each problem:

1. *Try to spot what skill is being tested.* For example, when you're asked to solve for x in the equation: $1 + 2 + 3 + 4 + 5 + 6 = 3 + 7 + x$; notice that by grouping the 1 with the 2, and the 3 with the 4, on the left side of the equation it becomes clear that x is just $5 + 6$. This isn't just an exercise in math skills. When you can see what skill a problem tests, you'll be able to answer the question faster and more accurately.

2. *Do the problem completely.* Too often, someone studying for the test will skip a problem, thinking, "I can do that," only to find out during the actual exam that the problem wasn't as simple as it looked. If you find a problem in this book easy, do it quickly, fill in the answer, and just look to see if you got it right. Then go on to the next problem.

3. *If you get a problem wrong, stop.* Use the discussion to figure out what you didn't know but needed to. If it's a theorem or a definition, memorize it. Remember, these problems come from the exams; you will see the same skill tested again.

4. *Also, when you get a problem wrong circle the problem number in the Concept-to-Problem index, on page 161.* Having done this, when you're through with each exam you can look and see what topic areas you're having the most trouble with and focus your attention on those.

When you're done with each test, you should:

1. *Be comfortable with the exam format.* This is important. When test day comes around you don't want to have to learn the peculiarities of "gridding-in" an answer.

2. *Have gained insight into what your individual strengths and weaknesses are.* If you diligently marked the problems you got wrong in the *Concept-to-Problem* index, you will be able to read off the number of problems you answered incorrectly for each problem category.

3. *Identify those skills that you're having difficulty with and:*

   • Use the *Concept-to-Problem* index to find and rework the problems that test the skill

   • Review your math textbook

   • Work through a "test-prep" book, such as *SAT Success* or *ACT Assessment Success*; or,

   • Ask your teacher for additional practice problems.

   Whatever method you choose to learn the material, having gone through *In-A-Flash: Math* enables you to focus on just those areas that need work.

4. *Keep Practicing.* The more problems you do, the more familiar you'll be with the exams and the skills they test. No question, this familiarity will get you a higher score.

Despite changes to the SAT over the years, its purpose and method are still basically the same as always:

1. The SAT math section tests your Arithmetic, Algebra I, and Geometry skills.

2. There are 60 (50 on the PSAT) questions consisting of 35 five-choice questions (25 on the PSAT), 15 quantitative comparison questions, and 10 grid-ins.

3. You have roughly one minute per problem.

The ACT Assessment Mathematics exam hasn't changed much over the years:

1. The ACT Assessment covers Algebra, Coordinate and Plane Geometry, and Trigonometry skills.

2. There are 60 multiple-choice questions.

3. You have roughly one minute per question.

Good luck. The first test begins on page 19.

STRATEGIES THAT REALLY WORK

Focus on What's Actually Being Asked

Read the question carefully and make sure you know the answer being sought.

Most ACT Assessment and SAT math problems will include a series of interrelated facts. The kinds of facts will vary depending on the kind of question.

In a word problem, these facts might include the speed of a train, the distance between two cities, and the time when the train leaves the station.

In a geometry problem, the facts might include the degree measures of two angles in a triangle, the length of one side of the triangle, and the diameter of a circle in which the triangle is inscribed.

In a graph-reading problem, the facts might include an entire series of numbers as depicted in the graph: monthly inches of rainfall in a particular county over a one-year period, for example.

One key to tackling any of these kinds of problems is to make sure you know which fact is being asked about and what form the answer should take. If you read hastily, you may *assume* a particular question when, in fact, the test-makers want to focus on a different one. Rather than asking about when the train will arrive at City B, they may ask when the train will reach the one-third point of the trip. Rather than asking about the area of either the triangle or the circle, they may ask instead about the area of the odd-shaped shaded region that falls between them. And rather than asking about the amount of rainfall in any particular month, they may ask about the *difference* among two of the months—a number that doesn't appear directly on the graph itself.

When in Doubt, Try Something

Occasionally, you'll find yourself staring at a problem without knowing how to begin solving it. If you're at a loss . . . try something. Often the numbers stated in the problem will suggest a starting point—by reminding you of operations and procedures you often used in math class.

If fractions are involved, for example, try simplifying them to the simplest form or multiply them out to rename them as whole numbers.

Or rename them as decimals or percentages if they lend themselves easily to that process (for example, $\frac{1}{10} = 10\%$).

If a geometry diagram appears, work from what you know (such as the degree measures of certain angles) to fill in information you don't know: the complementary angle alongside the angle that's marked, for example, or the angle on the other side of the transversal which must be equal to the angle you know.

If you're given a problem involving probability or permutations (varying combinations of things), just start listing all the possibilities.

Quite often, seemingly random experimenting like this will lead you quickly toward the right answer. Why? Because of the peculiar way in which ACT Assessment and SAT math problems are designed. The test-makers want to test you on a wide array of math topics in a short period of time. That means they want to ask you lots of questions that you can do quickly—in just about a minute each. Therefore, the questions are written so that the numbers themselves are generally "obvious." What's tricky is the underlying connection among the numbers. As soon as you "see" that connection, the math is usually simple.

As a result, ACT Assessment and SAT math tends to reward students who are willing to "mess around" with the numbers in the problem until an insight into the solution emerges. Once that "Aha!" moment happens, the answer is usually close at hand.

Round Off and "Guesstimate" Freely

It's not always necessary to work with exact numbers in solving the math problems in the ACT Assessment and in the multiple-choice and quantitative comparison sections of the SAT. Sometimes the fastest and even the most accurate way to an answer is to guesstimate. Here's an example:

> Juanita earns a weekly salary of $960. She is scheduled to receive a 10% salary increase next year and a 5% increase the year after that. What will her new weekly salary be?
>
> (A) $975.00
> (B) $1,104.00
> (C) $1,108.80
> (D) $1,920.00
> (E) $2,064.00

If you understand the logic behind this question, the calculations aren't difficult. You need to figure out the answer in two steps. First, add 10 percent to Juanita's current salary of $960. (This gives a result of $960 + $96 = $1,056.) Then add 5 percent of the larger salary ($1,056 + $52.80 = $1,108.80). Using either your calculator or pencil and paper, the math isn't hard; the right answer, as you see, is choice (C).

However, a situation could arise in which you haven't time to perform the precise calculations. For example, the proctor may have just announced "Five more minutes to go," and you have 10 more math items to complete. Under those circumstances, guesstimating is a useful strategy.

Here's how you'd approach the question. Juanita's starting salary is a little under $1,000. An additional 10 percent will be a little less than $100 (you should be able to figure that out in your head, just by moving the decimal point one space to the left). That brings her salary up to something under $1,100. Another five percent will bring it to a little over $1,100—making either answer B or C clearly correct.

You now have a 50 percent chance of guessing correctly, having spent just a few seconds on the question. (The correct answer is C.)

Here's another example of how rounding off and guesstimating can work:

A radio that normally sells for $59.95 is on sale for 30% off. What is the sale price, to the nearest dollar?

(A) $18
(B) $27
(C) $39
(D) $42
(E) $48

Again, you can take the time to work this out precisely—if you *have* the time. But if you're pressed, it's easy to guesstimate the best answer. Notice that $59.95 is very close to $60—a nice, round number that's simple to work with. You need to deduct 30% from $60. Now, you may be able to figure out, in your head, that 30% of $60 is $18. If not, you may be able to "see" that 30% is a little less than one third. One third of $60 is $20; so the discount offered during the sale is a little less than $20. You might guess $18 or $19. Either way, $42—choice (D)—is clearly the best answer.

Rounding off and guesstimating isn't necessary on most ACT Assessment and SAT items; in some cases, the numbers used are so few and so simple that you might as well work with them directly. But chances are you'll encounter several problems on every exam that will be made easier and quicker by guesstimating.

If Stymied, Plug In an Answer and Work Backward

On some questions, a quick route to the answer will jump out at you within a few seconds. In other cases, experimenting in some obvious way with the numbers will quickly direct you toward a solution. If neither of these methods works, try grabbing an answer from the five multiple-choice options and plugging it into the question. This will often lead you to the right answer quickly.

Here's an example:

During the first weekend after the opening of a certain new movie, ticket sales for the movie total $72 million. Each subsequent weekend, ticket sales decline by the same fraction. If ticket sales during the fourth weekend after the opening total $21 million, what is that fraction?

(A) $\frac{1}{4}$

(B) $\frac{1}{3}$

(C) $\frac{1}{2}$

(D) $\frac{2}{3}$

(E) $\frac{3}{4}$

The fastest way to a solution is to plug in an answer. Try choice (C), and see what happens. If ticket sales decline by $\frac{1}{2}$ with each passing weekend, then on the second weekend, sales will be half of $72 million—$36 million.

On the third weekend, sales will be half of $36 million, which is $18 million. *Stop!* The problem says that ticket sales will be $21 million during the *fourth* weekend. Obviously, if the sales are less than that during the *third* weekend, they'll be way too low during the fourth! So choice (C) cannot be the answer.

We can see that the weekly decline in ticket sales is less than $\frac{1}{2}$. The correct answer must then be a smaller fraction, meaning either choice (A) or choice (B). If you're pressed for time, choose one and move on; you have a 50% chance of being right. If you have time, plug in either and see whether it works. If you do, you'll see that choice (B) is correct.

Would it be possible to develop a formula to answer this question? Probably—some movie executive with an MBA has done it, I'll bet. But it would be crazy to try to devise a formula for the exam. Remember the unique advantage of a test like the ACT Assessment: *All the correct answers have been provided.* When it's not obvious which one is correct, pick one and try it. Even if the one you pick first is wrong, this method will usually let you pinpoint the best choice fairly quickly.

For Word Problems, Build an Equation That Will Yield the Answer You Want

For some students, word problems pose the toughest math challenge. You know the kind: They deal with planes traveling at a certain speed, pipes filling vats with liquid at a particular rate, workers painting walls at so many square feet per hour, and so on.

Curiously enough, in most word problems, the math itself is not difficult. You may have a couple fractions to multiply or divide or a simple equation to solve, but the computations will be easy. What's tricky is setting up the math in the first place—in other words, turning the words into numbers and symbols. Here are some pointers that will help.

LET THE UNKNOWN QUANTITY EQUAL WHAT YOU WANT TO SOLVE FOR

If the question asks "What fraction of the entire job will be completed after three hours?" begin writing your equation with $J =$, where J represents that fraction of the job. Conversely, if the question asks, "How many hours will it take to do $\frac{3}{7}$ of the entire job?," begin your equation with H, which should equal the hours of work needed. This way, once you've solved the equation, you automatically have your answer, with no further conversions needed.

BREAK THE PROBLEM DOWN INTO PHRASES, AND TRANSLATE EACH INTO A NUMERICAL EXPRESSION

Word problems can be intimidating because of their length and complexity. Your strategy: Divide and conquer. Break the problem into its component parts, and give each an appropriate number or symbol. Then devise an equation or formula that describes the relationship among these parts, and go ahead with the math.

Here's an example, using one typical kind of word problem—an age problem:

> Paul is eight years older than Sarah. Four years ago, Sarah was half the age Paul is now. How old is Sarah now?

First, notice that what you're looking for is Sarah's age now. So try to set up your equation making S (Sarah's age now) the unknown for which you will solve. The only other letter we'll need is P, which stands for Paul's age now.

Now create a couple simple equations that state in symbols and numbers what the sentences in the problem say.

"Paul is eight years older than Sarah" becomes: $P - 8 = S$.

"Four years ago, Sarah was half the age Paul is now" becomes $S - 4 = \frac{P}{2}$. To get rid of the fraction (usually a good idea), multiply this equation through by 2: $2S - 8 = P$.

Now you can solve for S by substituting the expression $2S - 8$ for P in the first equation:

$$(2S - 8) - 8 = S$$
$$2S - 16 = S$$
$$-16 = -S$$
$$S = 16$$

So Sarah's age today is 16. (Paul is 24.)

Table 5.1
Words and Phrases With Mathematical Translations

Equals	*is, amounts to, is the same as*
Addition	*and, with, along with, added to, in addition to, increased by, more than, greater than, larger than*
Subtraction	*less than, fewer than, without, take away, difference, decreased by, reduced by, smaller than*
Multiplication	*times, each, per, by, of, product*
Division	*divided by, part of, fraction, piece, portion*

Check out Table 5.1, which gives you some of the most common translations of words and phrases into mathematical operations. Learn the list—it'll work as a kind of "foreign phrasebook" for turning English into numbers on the exam.

CONVERT ALL QUANTITIES INTO UNITS THAT ARE EASIER TO WORK WITH

Don't feel locked into the numbers presented in the problem. If you can see that a different number you can easily get to will be simpler to work with, go for it by renaming the units of measurement.

In particular, when you can, look for opportunities to rename working units as the units in which the answer is wanted. So, for example, if you see that the answers are all stated in terms of square feet, while one of the numbers in the problem is in square yards, rename it as square feet before beginning your work. (One square yard equals nine square feet.)

ON GEOMETRY PROBLEMS, MINE THE DIAGRAM FOR CLUES TO THE ANSWER

Most geometry problems on the ACT Assessment and SAT are accompanied by diagrams. They are set up this way for a reason. You can usually leap from what you know—the facts you are given—to what you need to know simply by using the parts of the diagram as "stepping stones." Here's an example:

In the figure below, *A* and *B* are points on circle *O*. If the circumference of the circle is 12π, how much longer is arc *AB* than a straight line connecting the two points?

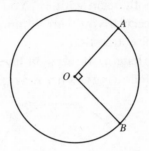

(A) 12π − 6

(B) 6π − $\sqrt{2}$

(C) 3π − 6

(D) 3π − 6$\sqrt{2}$

(E) π − $\sqrt{2}$

Solving a geometry problem like this one is a matter of working methodically. Just fill in the blank parts of the diagram using what you can deduce from the information you're given. (Use your pencil to mark the new facts right in the question booklet.) After you get to the fact being asked about, you're home free.

Here's how you'd apply the method to this item. First, note what you're being asked: "how much longer" one distance is as compared with another. In other words, what is the difference between the two lengths? Whenever a question asks about a difference, you should quickly think "subtraction"—and, sure enough, each of the answer choices includes a subtraction sign. To find the difference between the two lengths, you'll need to subtract the shorter length from the longer. Thus, solving the problem means figuring out what each of those lengths equals.

First, the longer of the two. The problem tells you that the circumference of the circle is 12π. The arc *AB* is a part of this circumference. How can you find its length? Just apply three basic geometric facts you should know: (1) The degree measure of an entire circle is 360; (2) An arc has a degree measure equal to that of the central angle that intercepts it; (3) A right angle has a degree measure of 90 degrees.

Based on these facts, you can see that the degree measure of arc *AB* is 90 degrees. That makes it one quarter of the entire circle; so its length must be one quarter the circumference of the circle, or 3π. Note that answers (C) and (D) both begin with 3π. You can already tell that one of these is probably correct. If you were running out of time, choose one and move on to the next question.

Now, the shorter length: the straight line from *A* to *B*. Draw it in on the diagram (see the following). What new geometric figure is created?

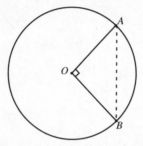

Of course, it's right triangle *AOB*. Not only that: It's a special kind of right triangle you ought to know, an *isosceles right triangle,* since it has two legs of equal length. In such a triangle, the ratio of lengths of the three sides is $1 - 1 - \sqrt{2}$, with $\sqrt{2}$ representing the hypotenuse. Thus, the length of $\overline{AB}$ will be equal to the length of either leg times $\sqrt{2}$.

What's the length of either leg? It's the same as a radius of the circle. We can figure that out from the formula for the circumference of the circle: $2\pi r$. Since $2\pi r = 12\pi$ (in this case), we can see that $2r = 12$, so the radius must have a length of 6. Therefore, $\overline{AB}$ has a length of $6\sqrt{2}$. When we subtract this from 3π, we get the difference in the two lengths: $3\pi - 6\sqrt{2}$, which is answer choice (D).

In some geometry questions, studying the diagram can make "math" totally unnecessary:

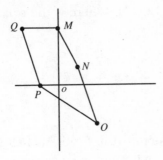

In the figure above, which two sides of polygon *MNOPQ* have the same slope?

(A) $\overline{MN}$ and $\overline{OP}$
(B) $\overline{NO}$ and $\overline{PQ}$
(C) $\overline{NO}$ and $\overline{OP}$
(D) $\overline{OP}$ and $\overline{QM}$
(E) $\overline{PQ}$ and $\overline{QM}$

When you studied coordinate geometry in school, you learned that the slope of a line is often expressed as a fraction. You also learned a formula for calculating the slope of a line from its endpoints. It's possible you may need to use that formula for one question on the test.

However, *the formula is totally unnecessary for this problem— and so are any numbers whatsoever.* You can tell which two sides have the same slope just by looking at the diagram and deciding which two sides of the polygon "go in the same direction." It's easy—the only possibility is choice (B), $\overline{NO}$ and $\overline{PQ}$, which are obviously parallel to one another.

As long as you have even a vague idea as to what the word *slope* means, you can scarcely get this question wrong. The diagram does all the work for you.

If No Diagram is Given, Sketch One

Sometimes, a question without a diagram simply cries out for one. That's what your pencil is for—and that's also why the test-makers kindly leave a generous margin of blank space on most pages of the exam. Draw your own diagram and read the answer right off it.

Here's an example.

In the standard (x,y) coordinate plane, three corners of a square are $(2,3)$, $(-1,0)$, and $(2,-3)$. Where is the square's fourth corner?

(A) $(-1,3)$
(B) $(1,-3)$
(C) $(2,0)$
(D) $(3,-2)$
(E) $(5,0)$

Can you picture this figure in your head? Me neither. Without a diagram, this problem is difficult; with one, it's very easy. Just use the margin of your test booklet to quickly sketch the (x,y) coordinate plane. Include enough space around the O point—the origin—to fit all of the three points named in the problem, and mark their location as indicated. Your sketch should look something like the following figure.

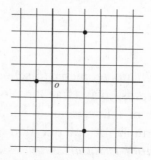

You can see that the square is set diagonally into the grid, with adjacent points separated from one another by three diagonal spaces. The fourth, missing corner is off to the right, at the point designated $(5,0)$ (see the following figure).

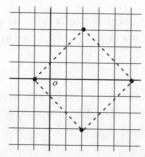

Thus, the answer is choice (E).

Avoid Lengthy Calculations and Working with Big Numbers

We've already seen examples of how straightforward are the mathematical computations on the ACT Assessment and SAT. You can count on this format. In fact, if you find yourself getting involved in long, complicated, or tricky calculations—especially ones using big numbers—stop working! You've probably overlooked a shortcut or trick that would make the calculations unnecessary.

Here's an example:

Students in a chemistry class were asked to rate the teacher on a scale from 1 to 5. 10% of the students gave the teacher a rating of 1; 30% gave a rating of 2; 40% gave a rating of 3; 15% gave a rating of 4, and 5% gave a rating of 5. What was the average of the ratings given?

(A) 1.85
(B) 2.40
(C) 2.75
(D) 3.25
(E) 3.50

There are several ways you could solve this problem. One way would be to assume a certain number of students in the class and then perform a series of multiplications to figure out the "total rating." If there were 100 students in the class, for example (a nice round number), then 10 would have given a rating of 1 ($10 \times 1 = 10$), 30 would have given a rating of 2 ($30 \times 2 = 60$), and so on. You'd find that the total rating is 275, which, when divided by 100 (the number of students in the class) gives you an average rating of 2.75.

However, none of this figuring is necessary. Instead, look at the pattern of ratings. More ratings of 3 were given than any other, with 2 a close second. The remaining ratings—a relatively low number, at that—were scattered among 1, 4, and 5. Based on these facts alone, and with no actual calculations, you could have concluded that the average rating would fall somewhere between 2.0 and 3.0, and that the average would probably be closer to 3.0 than to 2.0 (since more 3s than 2s were given). Only answer (C) fits those criteria.

Still somewhat unconvinced? Make a simple table of the ratings, like this:

Rating	1	2	3	4	5
Percentage	10	30	40	15	5

Now imagine that this scale is a kind of seesaw, with the middle value, 3, being the fulcrum on which the whole thing balances. It happens that more ratings fall at that middle value than at any other—so the largest "weight" is sitting right at the balancing point. Then, consider: on which end of the seesaw—the lower end or the higher end—is there more weight? Obviously, the lower end; in fact, there are exactly twice as many ratings in the 1/2 region as there are in the 4/5 region. Thus, the seesaw will "tip" toward the lower end—though not completely, since the plurality of ratings still fall smack in the middle. Again, you can see that the average rating will be just a little below 3.0.

The lesson: Avoid long calculations, and especially shun working with big numbers. The test-makers usually don't want you to mess with them. On many items, you can "see" the correct answers without having to do much figuring.

Use Your Calculator Sparingly

If you're used to working with a calculator, by all means bring your favorite to the test. You'll be happy you did if you blank out in the middle of the exam and forget what 8×7 equals.

If you're smart, however, you'll be very selective in using the calculator. Most students should touch the calculator on only one question out of four—or less. Here are the reasons why.

- Math questions on the ACT Assessment are specifically designed *not* to require a calculator. As we've explained, the exam focuses on mathematical reasoning, not on your ability to perform computations.

- It's easy to hit the wrong key, hit the right key twice instead of once, or make other mistakes when using a calculator, especially when you are hurriedly working with big numbers. (Ever get a wrong number on the phone? Everyone has. It's even easier with the small, flimsy buttons on most calculators.)

- You may be lulled into a false sense of security because you rely on the accuracy of the machine. Therefore, you may overlook a math mistake you'd otherwise spot.

- If you *do* suspect a math error when using your calculator, it's impossible to retrace your steps, since there are no notes or figures to check. (Calculators that print on paper are forbidden on the ACT Assessment and SAT.)

Don't get us wrong; a calculator can be a useful tool. But don't lean on it too heavily. If you find yourself working the calculator on all or even most questions, you're overdoing it. Put it aside, and grab it only when it's really necessary.

Most important: Start work on each question *without* the calculator in hand. The key is to decide what the question is asking, what information you have, and how to get from here to there. Only after you've figured these things out should you start calculating—if you must.

This section consists of 25 problems and five possible answer choices for each. For each problem, select the answer choice that represents the best solution and shade the corresponding oval.

1. A half hour can be divided into 30 1-minute periods or 1 30-minute period. Into how many other same size periods can you divide a half hour if each period must be an integer number of minutes?

   (A) 2
   (B) 3
   (C) 4
   (D) 5
   (E) 6

Note: Figure not drawn to scale.
$x < 90°$

2. Which of the following best describes a?

   (A) $3 < a < 4$
   (B) $a = 1$
   (C) $a = 5$
   (D) $1 < a < 5$
   (E) $1 < a < 7$

1. Ⓐ Ⓑ Ⓒ Ⓓ Ⓔ

2. Ⓐ Ⓑ Ⓒ Ⓓ Ⓔ

Answer #1: (E)

Formula: • 30 = 2 × 3 × 5

Concept: • Factoring and prime factors

You are asked the different ways of dividing 30 into integer parts. Dividing something into even portions suggests a solution that uses prime factors. Assuming you haven't memorized the prime factors of 30, your first step is to compute them. Looking at 30, you should immediately recognize that it is divisible by 10: 30 = 3 × 10. Three is the first prime factor. 10 = 2 × 5, each of which are primes, so the prime factors of 30 are 2, 3, and 5.

Any divisor of 30 will be the product of the prime factors of 30, so you must now construct all of the products of the prime factors of 30. I like to do this in ascending order. First off, 2 and 3 are clearly factors, in fact they are prime factors: 2 × 15 = 3 × 10 = 30. Is 4? No, because there is no way of generating a 4 by multiplying 2, 3, and 5. The next factor is 5, a prime factor: 5 × 6 = 30.

You can stop checking after 5 and 6 because any number greater than 5 that can divide 30 must do so fewer than 6 times and we've checked all of the positive integers less than 6. So, 2, 3, and 5 are divisors of 30, as well as 15, 10, and 6 (the numbers by which 2, 3, and 5 have to be multiplied to generate 30). There are 6 ways of dividing 30 into integer portions.

Answer #2: (D)

Formulas: • In a triangle, the sum of the lengths of two sides is greater than the length of the third side.
• Pythagorean theorem: $a^2 + b^2 = c^2$

Concept: • Triangle geometry

Because the figure is not drawn to scale, you should feel free to re-draw the unconstrained aspects of the picture. Imagine the extreme case where x is very small. In this case you'd have a picture like A:

A   B

As x shrinks, a approaches the difference between the two other sides: $4 - 3 = 1$.

At the other extreme, imagine case B with the side of length 3 being stretched out almost, but not quite, perpendicular to the side of length 4—it can't be exactly perpendicular because you are told $x < 90°$.

By applying the Pythagorean theorem, as x approaches a right angle, a^2 approaches $3^2 + 4^2 = 5^2$. So a can get as large as, but not equal to, 5.

3. What mathematical expression describes the product of two numbers being divided by their difference?

(A) $\dfrac{xy}{x-y}$

(B) $\dfrac{x+y}{x-y}$

(C) $\dfrac{x-y}{xy}$

(D) $\dfrac{xy}{x+y}$

(E) $\dfrac{x-y}{x+y}$

4. $\left(x - \dfrac{1}{x}\right)^2 + 4 =$

(A) 4

(B) 5

(C) $x^2 - \left(\dfrac{1}{x}\right)^2 + 4$

(D) $x^2 + \left(\dfrac{1}{x}\right)^2$

(E) $\left(x + \dfrac{1}{x}\right)^2$

3. Ⓐ Ⓑ Ⓒ Ⓓ Ⓔ

4. Ⓐ Ⓑ Ⓒ Ⓓ Ⓔ

Answer #3: Ⓐ

Concept: • Word problems

This problem tests your ability to create a mathematical expression from an English one. The method here is to work phrase by phrase. From the problem,

You read:	*You write:*
1. The product of two numbers	xy
2. being divided by	$\dfrac{xy}{}$
3. their difference	$\dfrac{xy}{x-y}$

Answer #4: Ⓔ

Formulas: • $\left(x + \dfrac{1}{x}\right)^2 = x^2 + 2 + \left(\dfrac{1}{x}\right)^2$

• $\left(x - \dfrac{1}{x}\right)^2 = x^2 - 2 + \left(\dfrac{1}{x}\right)^2$

• FOIL (First, Outer, Inner, Last)

Concept: • Polynomial arithmetic

The quantities $\left(x + \dfrac{1}{x}\right)^2$ and $\left(x - \dfrac{1}{x}\right)^2$ arise often in SAT problems because a) they look complicated with an x in the denominator of a fraction; and b) the middle term lacks an x.

To solve this problem, start with the $\left(x - \dfrac{1}{x}\right)^2$. Expand it out to get $x^2 - 2 + \left(\dfrac{1}{x}\right)^2$. Now, add 4 to the middle term to get $x^2 + 2 + \left(\dfrac{1}{x}\right)^2$. You should now be able to recognize this as $\left(x + \dfrac{1}{x}\right)^2$.

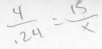

5. If the cost of a 4-minute telephone call is $0.24, then the cost of a 15-minute call at the same rate is:

   (A) $0.60
   (B) $0.65
   (C) $0.75
   (D) $0.90
   (E) $1.11

6. At a carnival, a booth is set up with a game that costs 15¢ to play. The first person to play wins a penny, the second person a nickel, the third person a dime, and the fourth a quarter. The cycle is repeated with the fifth person winning a penny and so on. After 43 people have played the game how much money has the booth made, net profit?

   (A) $2.06
   (B) $2.19
   (C) $3.00
   (D) $4.30
   (E) $6.45

5. (A) (B) (C) (D) (E)

6. (A) (B) (C) (D) (E)

Answer #5: Ⓓ

Formula: • Rate = $\dfrac{\text{Amount}}{\text{Time}}$

Concept: • Rates

There are many ways to approach this problem. One method is to set up the equivalence, "4 minutes is to 24¢ as 15 minutes is to x¢." As an equation, this looks like:

$$\frac{4 \text{ minutes}}{24¢} = \frac{15 \text{ minutes}}{x¢}$$

Cross multiplying and then solving for x you get:

$4x = 24 \times 15$

$x = 6 \times 15$

$x = 90¢$

Notice that by factoring out common divisors you can reduce the size of your numbers before multiplying. This helps reduce the chance of error.

Answer #6: Ⓑ

Formula: • In a sequence that repeats after n items, every item whose position is divisible by n will be the same as the nth item.

Concept: • Repeating sequences☆

The first person pays 15¢ and wins a penny, so the booth earns 14¢. The second person pays 15¢ and wins a nickel, so the booth earns 10¢. Likewise, the booth earns 5¢ from the third person and loses 10¢ from the fourth person. Then the cycle repeats. So each cycle through the game, the booth earns: 14¢ + 10¢ + 5¢ − 10¢ = 19¢.

The problem asks for how much money is made after 43 people have played the game. 43 is not divisible by 4 so let's look at the 40th person, the previous number divisible by 4. After the 40th person has played, the booth has been through 10 complete cycles. Having earned 19¢ per cycle, the booth has netted $1.90 profit. The booth earns 14¢ off the 41st player, bringing the profit to $2.04, then 10¢ and 5¢ from the 42nd and 43rd players, bringing the total profit to $2.19.

☆ See Concept-to-Problem Index page 141.

7. If $x - y = 10$, then
   $x - (2 - y) =$

   (A) 8
   (B) 10
   (C) 12
   (D) 18
   (E) cannot be determined

A is the set of integers evenly divisible by 2.

B is the set of integers evenly divisible by 3.

C is the set of integers evenly divisible by 6.

8. Which of the following numbers is contained within the intersection of A, B, and C?

   (A) 220
   (B) 221
   (C) 222
   (D) 224
   (E) 225

7. Ⓐ Ⓑ Ⓒ Ⓓ Ⓔ

8. Ⓐ Ⓑ Ⓒ Ⓓ Ⓔ

Answer #7: (E)

Formula: • $a - (b - c) = a - b + c$.

Concepts: • Arithmetic
• Pick and chooses$^{☆}$

Every SAT I've ever seen has at least one question that tests your ability to remove parentheses preceded by a subtraction sign. In this case, $x - (2 - y) = x - 2 + y$.

From $x - y = 10$, you know nothing about $x + y$, so you can't simplify the second expression.

If you're not sure that an answer can't be determined, try picking numbers that satisfy the first equation. If they yield different values in the second equation you are guaranteed that "cannot be determined" is the correct answer.

For example, let x be 10 and y be 0. This clearly satisfies the first equation. Plugging these values into the second equation yields $10 - (2 - 0) = 8$. Now let x be 11 and y be 1. These values also satisfy the first equation. However, they yield $11 - (2 - 1) = 10$ for the value of the second equation.

Because two sets of numbers that satisfy the first equation yield different values for the second equation, there is no fixed value for the second expression.

Answer #8: (C)

Theorems: • All numbers divisible by 2 end in either 0, 2, 4, 6, or 8.
If a number is divisible by 3, then the sum of its digits is divisible by 3.

Concepts: • Factoring and prime factors
• Arithmetic

Choices (B) and (E) end in 1 and 5, respectively, so they are not divisible by 2, not in set A, and consequently not in the intersection of the three sets.

The digits of choices (A) and (D) add up to 4 and 8, respectively. Neither of these is divisible by 3, so they are not in set B and consequently not in the intersection of sets A, B, and C.

We know that 222 is in set A because it ends in a 2 and therefore is divisible by 2. We know that 222 is in set B because the sum of its digits is 6, which is divisible by 3. Finally, we know that 222 is in set C because any number divisible by both 2 and 3 is divisible by 6.

9. 30% of 80 is what percent of 24?

(A) 44
(B) 50
(C) 56
(D) 66
(E) 100

10. Because of bad weather, a traveler could average 40 miles per hour during a 240-mile trip from city A to city B. Coming back, she was able to average 60 miles per hour. What was her overall average speed measured in miles per hour?

(A) 45
(B) 48
(C) 50
(D) 52
(E) 55

9. Ⓐ Ⓑ Ⓒ Ⓓ Ⓔ

10. Ⓐ Ⓑ Ⓒ Ⓓ Ⓔ

Answer #9: Ⓔ

Formula: • $x\%$ of $y = \dfrac{x}{100}y$

Concepts: • Percentages
• Word problems

Because this is a word problem, your first step is to convert it to an equation. This is most easily done phrase by phrase:

You read: *You write:*

1. 30% of 80 $\dfrac{30}{100} \times 80$

2. is $\dfrac{30}{100} \times 80 =$

3. what percent $\dfrac{30}{100} \times 80 = \dfrac{p}{100}$

4. of 24 $\dfrac{30}{100} \times 80 = \dfrac{p}{100} \times 24$

Now solve for p. Before doing any arithmetic, it's helpful to divide both sides of the equation by 100. This leaves you with $30 \times 80 = p \times 24$. Because $3 \times 8 = 24$, you next want to expand the left side of the equation to read:

$$3 \times 10 \times 8 \times 10 = p \times 24$$

Then you divide both sides of the equation by 24 to end up with $10 \times 10 = p$, or $p = 100$.

Answer #10: Ⓑ

Formula: • Rate $= \dfrac{\text{Amount}}{\text{Time}}$

Concept: • Rates

Rates can be tricky. If you drive 50 mph for an hour and 60 mph for an hour your average is 55 mph during the 2 hours. However, if you drive 50 mph for 30 miles and 60 mph for 30 miles, your average is NOT 55 mph. Why not? Because it took you longer to drive the first 30 miles.

In this problem, the woman drove 240 miles at 40 mph. This took her $\dfrac{240}{40} = 6$ hrs. Then the woman drove another 240 miles at 60 mph. This took her $\dfrac{240}{60} = 4$ hrs. The total time she spent driving was 6 hrs + 4 hrs = 10 hrs. The total distance she drove was 240 miles $\times$ 2 = 480 miles. So her average miles per hour was $\dfrac{480 \text{ miles}}{10 \text{ hours}} = 48$ mph.

11. If $x^2 + y^2 = 15$, and $xy = 5$, then $x + y =$

(A) 5 only
(B) −5 only
(C) 5 or −5
(D) 5 or 10
(E) 10 or −10

12. A woman jogs 6 miles at 4 miles per hour. At *approximately* what speed would she need to travel during the next $2\frac{1}{2}$ hours to have an average speed of 6 miles per hour during the complete trip?

(A) 4 mph
(B) 6 mph
(C) 7 mph
(D) 9 mph
(E) 10 mph

11. Ⓐ Ⓑ Ⓒ Ⓓ Ⓔ

12. Ⓐ Ⓑ Ⓒ Ⓓ Ⓔ

Answer #11: Ⓒ

Formulas:
- $(x + y)^2 = x^2 + 2xy + y^2$
- If $x^2 = y$, then $x = \sqrt{y}$ or $x = -\sqrt{y}$

Concept:
- Polynomial arithmetic

As you start this problem, if you notice that the question is asking for the value of $x + y$ and you notice that you have many of the components for determining the value of $(x + y)^2$, then you're on the right track. By reordering its terms, you can say that:

$$(x + y)^2 = x^2 + 2xy + y^2$$
$$= x^2 + y^2 + 2xy$$

Because you know that $x^2 + y^2 = 15$ and that $xy = 5$, you can substitute into your equation to get:

$$(x + y)^2 = 15 + 2(5)$$
$$= 25$$

Remember that every positive number has two square roots, a positive one and a negative one. In this case, $25 = (-5)^2 = (5)^2$. So, there are two possible values for $(x + y)$, -5, and 5.

Answer #12: Ⓒ

Formula:
- Rate $= \dfrac{\text{Amount}}{\text{Time}}$

Concepts:
- Rates
- Approximation☆

This problem breaks the woman's jog into two parts and gives you data about each part. Each time you know two out of three parameters in the rate equation. You must apply the equation to the different jog parts and to the whole, until you can solve for the rate at which the woman travels during the second part, $Rate_2$. Each of the following steps computes a missing piece.

You are told:
- $Dist_1 = 6$ miles
- $Rate_1 = 4$ mph
- $Time_2 = 2.5$ hours
- $Rate_w = 6$ mph

You compute:
- $Time_1 = Dist_1 \div Rate_1 = 6$ miles $\div$ 4 mph $= 1.5$ hrs
- $Time_w = Time_1 + Time_2 = 1.5$ hrs $+ 2.5$ hrs $= 4$ hrs
- $Dist_w = Rate_w \times Time_w = 6$ mph $\times$ 4 hrs $= 24$ miles
- $Dist_2 = Dist_w - Dist_1 = 24$ miles $- 6$ miles $= 18$ miles
- $Rate_2 = Dist_2 \div Time_2 = 18$ miles $\div$ 2.5 hrs $= 7.2$ mph

Because the problem asks for an approximate speed, you should round 7.2 to 7.

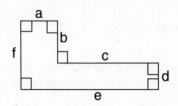

13. The area of the above figure is all of the following *except*:

(A) *ab + de*

(B) *af + cd*

(C) *fe – bc*

(D) *af + de*

(E) *ab + ad + cd*

14. If $(x - 2)(x + 2) =$ $(x - 2)^2$, then $x =$

(A) −4

(B) −2

(C) 0

(D) 2

(E) 4

13. Ⓐ Ⓑ Ⓒ Ⓓ Ⓔ

14. Ⓐ Ⓑ Ⓒ Ⓓ Ⓔ

Answer #13: Ⓓ

Formula: • Area of a Rectangle = Length × Width
Concept: • Rectangle geometry

The possible solutions to the problem all make use of the rectangles that make up the larger picture. This suggests that you should explicitly draw in those rectangles:

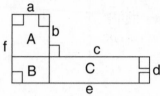

Now you can see more clearly that the total area of the figure is A + B + C. The first offered solution is *ab* + *de*. *ab* = A, and *de* = B + C, so *ab* + *de* = A + B + C, the total area of the figure. Continuing in this same fashion, all of the expressions in the possible solutions are equal to the area of the figure except D. Solution D is *af* + *ed*. *af* = A + B and *ed* = B + C, so *af* + *ed* = A + B + B + C. The rectangle with area B is counted twice; therefore, *af* + *de* is greater than, not equal to, the area of the original figure.

Answer #14: Ⓓ

Formula: • Division by 0 is undefined
Concept: • Polynomial arithmetic

When you first see this problem, you might notice that there's an $(x - 2)$ on both sides of the equation and divide it out, leaving: $x + 2 = x - 2$. Further simplifying what's left by subtracting an x from both sides you get $2 = -2$. Oops! In almost every case, this one included, if after doing a division you come up with one number equal to a different one, then you divided by zero.

In this case, because division by zero is not defined, when you divide both sides of the equation by $(x - 2)$ you must consider the case that $x = 2$ (i.e. $x - 2 = 0$). The simplest way to consider this case is to plug 2 in for x and see if you get a true statement. Plugging 2 in for x leaves you $(0)(4) = 0$, which is a true statement. So 2 is the correct solution.

15. The operation $\boxed{x}$ indicates that one should subtract 2 from x and then multiply the result by 2. The operation $\widehat{x}$ indicates that one should multiply x by 2 and then subtract 2 from the product. Therefore, $\widehat{x} - \boxed{x} =$

(A) −2
(B) 0
(C) 2
(D) 4
(E) cannot be determined from the given information

16. Joan can paint m meters of fence in h hours and 15 minutes. What is her average speed in meters per hour?

(A) $h\left(1 + \dfrac{1}{4}\right)m$

(B) $\dfrac{m}{h + 15}$

(C) $\dfrac{4m}{4h + 1}$

(D) $\dfrac{h + 15}{m}$

(E) $\dfrac{h + \dfrac{1}{4}}{m}$

15. Ⓐ Ⓑ Ⓒ Ⓓ Ⓔ

16. Ⓐ Ⓑ Ⓒ Ⓓ Ⓔ

Answer #15: (C)

Formula: • $a - b(c - d) = a - bc + bd$
Concepts: • Arithmetic
                 • Functions
                 • Word problems

Both $\boxed{x}$ and $\boxed{\hat{x}}$ are described in words. Your first step is to translate the words to mathematical expressions. To determine the value of $\boxed{x}$, as noted, you "subtract 2 and then multiply the result by 2." As a mathematical expression, this can be written $\boxed{x} = 2(x - 2)$. Likewise, to determine the value of $\boxed{\hat{x}}$, you "multiply by 2 and then subtract 2 from the product." As a mathematical expression, this can be written: $\boxed{\hat{x}} = (2x - 2)$.

Now, $\boxed{\hat{x}} - \boxed{x}$ can be written $(2x - 2) - 2(x - 2)$. Simplifying this expression, you get $2x - 2 - 2x + 4$, which is 2, choice (C).

When removing the second set of parentheses, don't forget to change the sign on the last 2 and to multiply both the x and the 2 inside the parentheses by the 2 outside of the parentheses. These are both common errors. In fact, they are the skills that you are being tested on in this problem.

Answer #16: (C)

Formulas: • 1 hour = 60 minutes
                 • Rate $= \dfrac{\text{Amount}}{\text{Time}}$
Concepts: • Unit conversions☆
                 • Fractions
                 • Rates

Because this problem asks for Joan's average speed in meters per hour, we know that we should convert the 15 minutes to 0.25 hours. The problem asks for the average painting rate so you need to divide the total length of fence, m meters, by the total time, $h + 0.25$ hours, to get $\dfrac{m}{h + 0.25}$. Although this is correct, it isn't one of the answer choices!

Before dismissing your solution, try simplifying it. Eliminate the 0.25 in the denominator of the fraction by multiplying numerator and denominator by 4. The result is $\dfrac{4m}{4h + 1}$.

17. If a woman is paid c dollars an hour for every hour she works up to 8 hours and is paid double for every hour she works after 8 hours, how many dollars will she be paid for working h hours, where $h > 8$?

(A) ch

(B) $\dfrac{h}{c}$

(C) $2ch - 8c$

(D) $ch + 8c$

(E) $2ch + 8$

18. If $x > y$ then the point (x,y) can be in all of the following areas of the coordinate axes *except:*

(A) Quadrant I

(B) Quadrant II

(C) Quadrant III

(D) Quadrant IV

(E) The x or y axes

17. Ⓐ Ⓑ Ⓒ Ⓓ Ⓔ

18. Ⓐ Ⓑ Ⓒ Ⓓ Ⓔ

Answer #17: Ⓒ

Formula: • $ = hours × rate
Concept: • Rates

This problem tests your ability to apply two salary rates. Because the total number of hours the woman worked, h, is greater than 8, she works the full 8 hours at the lesser salary rate. How many hours does she work at the greater rate? She has worked a total of h hours, 8 of them at the lesser salary rate, so the rest, $(h - 8)$, must be at the greater rate.

Now you know the amounts of time and the rates at which the woman worked, so you can apply the rate formula to determine how much she earned:

Total earnings = earnings during first 8 hrs.
           + earnings for work after 8 hrs
      = 8 times lesser rate
           + $(h - 8)$ times greater rate
      = $8c + (h - 8)2c$
      = $8c + 2ch - 16c$
      = $2cb - 8c$

Answer #18: Ⓑ

Definitions: • Quadrant
            • Coordinate axes
Concept: • Coordinate geometry

This is a good situation in which to draw a picture. The coordinate axes can be drawn as follows:

Now, add the line $y = x$. It's a line running diagonally from the lower left of the graph to the upper right at a 45° angle to the axes. Next, shade in the area of the graph to the right and below the line. This is the area in which $x > y$. The only quadrant with no shading is Quadrant II, choice (B).

Another way of looking at this problem is to say that in Quadrant II x is always negative and y is always positive. No negative number is greater than any positive number; so, in Quadrant II x can never be greater than y.

19. $\triangle ABC$ has angles of 30°, 45°, and 105°. If the side opposite the 30° angle has length $\sqrt{2}$, then the area of $\triangle ABC$ is:

(A) $\dfrac{1}{2} + \dfrac{\sqrt{3}}{2}$

(B) $2\sqrt{2}$

(C) $1 + \sqrt{3}$

(D) $\dfrac{1}{2} + \dfrac{\sqrt{6}}{2}$

(E) $\dfrac{\sqrt{2}}{2} + \sqrt{3}$

20. Over what interval(s) is the statement $x^3 < x^2$ true?

(A) all x

(B) $x > 0$

(C) $x > 1$ or $x < -1$

(D) $-1 < x < 1$

(E) $x > 1$

19. Ⓐ Ⓑ Ⓒ Ⓓ Ⓔ

20. Ⓐ Ⓑ Ⓒ Ⓓ Ⓔ

Answer #19: Ⓐ

Definitions: • In a 30-60-90 triangle, the lengths of the sides opposite the angles are in the ratio of $1 : \sqrt{3} : 2$
• In a 45-45-90 triangle, the lengths of the sides opposite the angles are in the ratio of $1 : 1 : \sqrt{2}$

Concept: • Triangle geometry

The first step in solving this problem is to draw the picture:

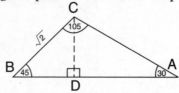

Now draw the perpendicular from C to $\overline{AB}$ and notice that you get a 45-45-90 and a 30-60-90 triangle.

Next, using the formula for 45-45-90 triangles, you can compute the lengths of $\overline{CD}$ and $\overline{BD}$, which are both 1.

Write these in. Using the formula for 30-60-90 triangles, you can see that the length of $\overline{AD}$ is $\sqrt{3}$.

The altitude of the triangle is 1 and the base is $1 + \sqrt{3}$. It follows that the area $\triangle ABC$ is $\dfrac{1}{2} + \dfrac{\sqrt{3}}{2}$, choice (A).

Answer #20: Ⓔ

Formula: • x^2 is non-negative for all x

Concepts: • Exponents
• Inequalities

You are being asked to solve the inequality $x^3 > x^2$.

Subtract x^2 from both sides: $x^3 - x^2 > 0$
Factor an x^2 out on the left: $x^2(x - 1) > 0$

Note that x cannot be 0 because the statement $x^3 < x^2$ is not true when x is 0. Also, x^2 is never negative, so you can divide both sides of the inequality by x^2 without having to worry about changing the direction of the inequality sign.

Divide both sides of the inequality by x^2: $x - 1 > 0$
Add 1 to both sides: $x > 1$

21. A six-sided, fair die is rolled 100 times. Which of the following statements must be true?

   I. At least one side lands face up at least 17 times.

   II. All sides land face up at least 16 times.

   III. Side one lands face up at least 2 times.

(A) None is true
(B) I only
(C) II only
(D) III only
(E) All are true

22. The sum of the squares of integers from 1 to n is equal to $\frac{1}{6}n(n + 1)(2n + 1)$. What is the average of the set of squares $\{1^2, 2^2, \ldots, 9^2\}$?

(A) 31

(B) $\dfrac{95}{3}$

(C) $\dfrac{95}{2}$

(D) 190

(E) 285

21. Ⓐ Ⓑ Ⓒ Ⓓ Ⓔ

22. Ⓐ Ⓑ Ⓒ Ⓓ Ⓔ

Answer #21: Ⓑ

Concept: • Probability

Probability problems on the SAT often test your ability to distinguish between valid and faulty statements. Usually, instead of calculating solutions, you will solve problems by creating examples of low probability situations that disprove statements. These situations often consist of one event happening every time or every event happening evenly.

In this problem you can create the situation that, as improbable as it might be, the die lands on side six every time. From this example you can immediately disprove statements II and III.

To disprove statement I you want to create a situation wherein each side of the die comes up no more than 16 times. If each side of a six-sided die lands face up 16 times, the die must have been rolled $6 \times 16 = 96$ times. Yet the die in the problem was rolled 100 times. These last four rolls must land on some side and that side has landed up at least 17 times; therefore, statement I is true, and it is the only one that must be true.

Answer #22: Ⓑ

Definition: • Average $= \dfrac{\text{Sum of the items in a list}}{\text{Number of items in the list}}$

Concept: • Averages

For this problem you're asked to find the average of the set of squares, n^2, for n from 1 to 9.

You're told that the sum of these numbers can be computed with the formula $\dfrac{1}{6}n(n + 1)(2n + 1)$. In this case, n is nine so you can write the sum as $\dfrac{1}{6}(9)(10)(19)$. You also know that there are 9 integers between 1 and 9 inclusive. So, you've got all of the pieces to compute the average:

$$\text{Average} = \dfrac{\dfrac{1}{6}(9)(10)(19)}{9}$$

$$= \dfrac{1}{6}(10)(19)$$

$$= \dfrac{190}{6}$$

$$= \dfrac{95}{3}$$

23. A square is inscribed in a circle in such a way that the vertices of the square touch the circle. If the square has side $a\sqrt{2}$, then the area of the circle is:

(A) $\frac{1}{4}\pi a^2$

(B) $\frac{1}{2}\pi a^2$

(C) πa^2

(D) $\sqrt{2}\pi a^2$

(E) $2\pi a^2$

24. A group of 9 friends invest equally in a business opportunity that costs $20,000. If n more friends were to take part evenly in the investment, which expression best describes how much less each of the original 9 would have to pay?

(A) $\dfrac{20,000}{9} - \dfrac{20,000}{n}$

(B) $\dfrac{20,000}{9} - \dfrac{20,000}{9 + n}$

(C) $\dfrac{20,000}{9 + n}$

(D) $\dfrac{20,000}{n}$

(E) $\dfrac{20,000}{9 - n}$

23. Ⓐ Ⓑ Ⓒ Ⓓ Ⓔ

24. Ⓐ Ⓑ Ⓒ Ⓓ Ⓔ

Answer #23: Ⓒ

Formulas:
- The length of the diagonal of a square with side s is $s\sqrt{2}$
- Area of a circle $= \pi r^2$

Concepts:
- Circle geometry
- Rectangle geometry

Start with a picture:

For this problem, begin with the fact that the square has side $a\sqrt{2}$ and compute the length of its diagonal:

$a\sqrt{2}\sqrt{2} = 2a$. Notice that the diagonals of the square are also diameters of the circle. The radius of the circle is half its diameter, so you can compute it to be a. Given the radius of the circle, you can compute the area of the circle: $A = \pi r^2 = \pi a^2$, choice (C).

Answer #24: Ⓑ

Concept:
- Word Problems

This problem type tests your ability to model a situation with mathematical expressions. Notice that you never have to do the arithmetic. To start this problem look at what's being asked for: "how much less each . . . would pay." How much less they would pay is the difference between what they would pay before and after the additional friends joined in.

Before the additional friends joined in, each friend had to pay one ninth of the $20,000 cost, or $\dfrac{20{,}000}{9}$ dollars. With the additional friends there are $9 + n$ people, so each person must pay $\dfrac{1}{9+n}$ of the $20,000, or $\dfrac{20{,}000}{9+n}$ dollars. The difference between the cost before and after is, therefore, choice (B): $\dfrac{20{,}000}{9} - \dfrac{20{,}000}{9+n}$.

25. If $.2^2 = \sqrt{x}$, then $x =$

    (A) .2

    (B) .02

    (C) .04

    (D) .016

    (E) .0016

25. Ⓐ Ⓑ Ⓒ Ⓓ Ⓔ

Answer #25: Ⓔ

Concepts: • Arithmetic
  • Exponents and square roots

This problem has two twists. First, the question mixes a square root, $\sqrt{x}$, and a square, $.2^2$. Many people, in a hurry, will toss out the exponent and the radical sign to get $.2 = x$, which is incorrect.

The second twist is raising a decimal to a power. Moving too quickly you might write $.2^2 = .4$. It's often easier to do arithmetic with fractions: $.2 = \dfrac{2}{10}$ and $.2^2 = \left(\dfrac{2}{10}\right)^2 = \dfrac{4}{100}$.

Squaring both sides of the original equation you get:

$$x = (.2^2)^2 = .2^4 = \left(\dfrac{2}{10}\right)^4 = \dfrac{16}{10^4} = .0016, \text{ choice (E)}.$$

Questions 26–40 each consist of two quantities, one in Column A and one in Column B. You are to compare the two quantities and on the answer sheet fill in:

(A)   if the quantity in Column A is greater
(B)   if the quantity in Column B is greater
(C)   if the two quantities are equal
(D)   if the relationship cannot be determined from the information given

AN (E) RESPONSE WILL NOT BE SCORED

NOTES:

1. In certain questions, information concerning one or both of the quantities to be compared is centered above the two columns.
2. In a given question, a symbol that appears in both columns represents the same thing in Column A as it does in Column B.
3. Letters such as x, n, and k stand for real numbers.

EXAMPLES		
	Column A	Column B
E1.	2×6	$2 + 6$
E2.	$180 - x$	y
E3.	$p - q$	$q - p$

For E2: $x°$ $y°$

E1. ● Ⓑ Ⓒ Ⓓ
E2. Ⓐ Ⓑ ● Ⓓ
E3. Ⓐ Ⓑ Ⓒ ●

26.

27.

$$y^2 = 36$$
$$x^2 = 25$$

Column A	Column B
The number of prime numbers between 1 and 100	The number of odd numbers between 1 and 100

Column A	Column B
x	y

26. (A) (B) (C) (D)

27. (A) (B) (C) (D)

Answer #26: (B)

Definitions: • Odd number: A number not divisible by 2
               • Prime number: A number with exactly 2 factors, namely 1
                 and itself

Concept: • Factoring and prime numbers

All primes (except 2) are odd. Many odd numbers, such as 9, 15, 21, and 25, are not prime, so there are many more odd numbers than primes between 1 and 100.

Answer #27: (D)

Concept: • Exponents and square roots

This problem tests whether you know that for most second degree equations—those with a variable raised to the power of 2—there are two solutions. In the first equation, $y^2 = 36$, the two solutions are $y = 6$ or $y = -6$.

If in this problem $y = 6$ and $x = -5$, then $y > x$. But if $y = -6$ and $x = 5$, then $x > y$. Consequently, you cannot determine the relationship between x and y for all cases, so the choice is (D).

28.

Column A	Column B
32	8.2×4.3

29.

$$x = 1 - \cfrac{1}{1 - \cfrac{1}{2}}$$

Column A	Column B
x	$\dfrac{1}{2}$

28. (A) (B) (C) (D)

29. (A) (B) (C) (D)

Answer #28: Ⓑ

Concepts: • Approximation☆
                  • Arithmetic

Being able to look at an arithmetic expression and have a rough idea of the answer is an important skill. This problem tests your ability to look at the expression 8.2×4.3 and notice quickly that it is a little more than 32.

How? You should recognize that $8 \times 4 = 32$. You also know that 8.2 is a little more than 8, and 4.3 is a little more than 4, so their product is a little more than 8×4 or 32. Notice that we never had to do the arithmetic or take the chance of making a multiplication error.

Now that the SAT allows you to use calculators you could have multiplied 8.2 and 4.3 using a calculator and compared the result (35.26) to 32. However, that also has the potential for error and probably isn't any faster than approximating.

Answer #29: Ⓑ

Definitions: • The reciprocal of x is $\dfrac{1}{x}$

                • $\dfrac{1}{a/b} = \dfrac{b}{a}$

Concept: • Fractions

Doing this problem one step at a time only involves knowing what $1 - \dfrac{1}{2}$ is (easy enough!) and how to compute the reciprocal of a fraction.

First, simplify the denominator of the larger fraction from $1 - \dfrac{1}{2}$ to just $\dfrac{1}{2}$. Now you're left with the equation $x = 1 - \dfrac{1}{1/2}$. If you know that the reciprocal of a fraction can be computed by "flipping over" the fraction, then you know that $\dfrac{1}{1/2} = 2$, and, consequently, you can further simplify the equation to read $x = 1 - 2$. Now finish solving to get $x = -1$. Column A, -1, is less than $\dfrac{1}{2}$, so the answer is B.

☆ See Concept-to-Problem Index page 161.

30.

Five years ago blue ribbon cost 20¢ more per yard than red ribbon.

Column A	Column B
The cost of red ribbon now	The cost of blue ribbon now

31.

Column A	Column B
The sum of the remainders when five consecutive numbers are divided by 5	5

30. Ⓐ Ⓑ Ⓒ Ⓓ

31. Ⓐ Ⓑ Ⓒ Ⓓ

Answer #30:   Ⓓ

Concept: • Irrelevant information☆

Knowing how to spot irrelevant information is one of several skills tested on the SAT.

   In this example, knowing the price of red and blue ribbon from five years ago tells you nothing about the price now. Maybe the cost of red dye skyrocketed; maybe neither price changed. In short, from the information given, you do not know the relationship between the cost of red ribbon now (Column A) and the cost of blue ribbon now (Column B), so the correct answer is (D).

Answer #31:   Ⓐ

Definition: • Remainder
Concept: • Arithmetic

Remainders have a lot of interesting properties. For example, when a number is divided by 5, the possible remainders are 0, 1, 2, 3, or 4. Furthermore, if a number is divided and has a remainder of 3, then the next consecutive number will have a remainder of 4 when divided by 5, and 5 will evenly divide the number after that (i.e., the remainder is 0).

   For this problem, you need to know that if any 5 consecutive numbers are is divided by 5 then the set of remainders must be 0, 1, 2, 3, and 4. Without doing the addition, you should notice that the sum of these numbers is greater than 5. Why? The set includes a 4 and a 3. The 4 and 3 add up to 7, which is greater than 5, so adding even more positive numbers only increases the total. Consequently, the value described in Column A is greater than 5, the value in Column B.

   As is often the case, by looking at the problem carefully before performing computations, you can often avoid doing arithmetic altogether and the possibility for miscalculation that goes along with it.

32.

n is a positive integer

Column A	Column B
$(-1)^n$	1^n

33.

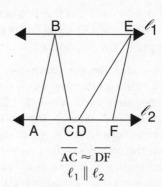

$$\overline{AC} \approx \overline{DF}$$
$$\ell_1 \parallel \ell_2$$

Column A	Column B
Area of $\triangle ABC$	Area of $\triangle DEF$

---

32. Ⓐ Ⓑ Ⓒ Ⓓ

33. Ⓐ Ⓑ Ⓒ Ⓓ

Answer #32: Ⓓ

Formulas:
- $(-1)^n = 1$, if n is an even number
- $(-1)^n = -1$, if n is an odd number

Concept:
- Exponents

Problems that involve raising -1 and 1 to powers occur often on the SAT because, unlike other numbers, -1 or 1 raised to a power is always 1 or -1.

The value in Column B, 1^n, equals 1 for every integer n. The value in Column A, $(-1)^n$, equals -1 if n is odd and 1 if n is even. In one case, the values in the two columns are equal; in the other case, the value in column B is greater. Because the only restriction on n is that it is positive, not that it is odd or even, you can't tell which case holds and therefore can't determine the relationship between the values in the two columns.

Answer #33: Ⓒ

Formulas:
- Area of a triangle $= \dfrac{1}{2} \times$ base $\times$ height
- The distance between parallel lines is the same at every point along the lines

Concept:
- Triangle geometry

Your goal is to determine the relationship between the areas of the two triangles ABC and DEF. If you can show that the corresponding bases and heights of the two triangles are equal, then you have shown that their areas are also equal.

You are given the fact that $\overline{AC} \approx \overline{DF}$, so you know the bases of $\triangle ABC$ and $\triangle DEF$ are equal. The corresponding altitudes to these bases are the perpendiculars between ℓ_1 and ℓ_2 that pass through points B and E. Because ℓ_1 and ℓ_2 are parallel, you know that the distance between them is the same wherever it is measured. Consequently, the altitudes of the two triangles are also equal.

Because both the bases and the altitudes of the two triangles are equal their areas must also be equal, so the correct answer is (C).

34. Let $\boxed{n}$ be defined by the equation $\boxed{n} = (n + 1)^2$

35.

Column A	Column B
$\dfrac{\boxed{8}}{\boxed{4}}$	$\boxed{2}$

Column A	Column B
$a\%$ of b	$b\%$ of a

34. Ⓐ Ⓑ Ⓒ Ⓓ

35. Ⓐ Ⓑ Ⓒ Ⓓ

Answer #34:   (B)

Concept: • Functions

In this problem, the fraction on the left becomes:

$\dfrac{(8 + 1)^2}{(4 + 1)^2}$. You can simplify this to be $\dfrac{9^2}{5^2}$, and further simplify it to be $\left(\dfrac{9}{5}\right)^2$.

Before simplifying Column A any further, look at Column B, which simplifies to $\boxed{2}$ = $(2 + 1)^2 = (3)^2$. Now you have $\left(\dfrac{9}{5}\right)^2$ in Column A and 3^2 in Column B. $\dfrac{9}{5}$ is pretty close to 2, so without doing any arithmetic you know that $\dfrac{9}{5} < 3$ and consequently $\left(\dfrac{9}{5}\right)^2 < 3^2$. Therefore, the value in Column B is greater than Column A.

Answer #35:   (C)

Formula: • $x\% = \dfrac{x}{100}$

Concept: • Percentages

You've probably been told many times that a percentage is shorthand for a fraction whose denominator is 100. So, "$x\%$ of something" is shorthand for saying $\dfrac{x}{100}$ multiplied by that thing.

Given this definition, we can rewrite "$a\%$ of b" from Column A as $\dfrac{a}{100} \times b$ $= \dfrac{ab}{100}$. We can also rewrite "$b\%$ of a" from Column B as $\dfrac{b}{100} \times a = \dfrac{ba}{100}$. Because multiplication is commutative—that is, $ab = ba$—we know that $\dfrac{ab}{100} = \dfrac{ba}{100}$. Therefore, the values in Columns A and B are equal for any a and b, and the correct answer is (C).

36.

$$t < s$$

Column A	Column B
The average of t and s	s

37.

Column A	Column B
The distance from the point (a, a) to the point (x, y) on the coordinate axes	The distance from the point (a, a) to the point (y, x) on the coordinate axes

36. Ⓐ Ⓑ Ⓒ Ⓓ

37. Ⓐ Ⓑ Ⓒ Ⓓ

Answer #36: (B)

Definition: • Average $= \dfrac{\text{sum of the items in a list}}{\text{number of items in the list}}$

Concept: • Averages

Given any two unequal numbers, their average has to be somewhere between them. Therefore, the average of t and s lies somewhere between t and s. Because t is less than s, you know that any number between t and s is less than s. Therefore, the value described in Column B is greater than the value in Column A.

Answer #37: (C)

Formula: • The distance between two points (x_1, y_1) and

(x_2, y_2) is $\sqrt{(x_2 - x_1)^2 + (y_2 - y_1)^2}$

Concept: • Coordinate geometry

To determine the value described in Column A, plug (a,a) for (x_1, y_1) and (x,y) for (x_2, y_2) into the distance equation to get $\sqrt{(x - a)^2 + (y - a)^2}$. Likewise, to determine the value described in Column B, plug in (a,a) for (x_1, y_1) and (y,x) for (x_2, y_2) to get $\sqrt{(y - a)^2 + (x - a)^2}$. The only difference between the two expressions is the order in which $(y - a)^2$ and $(x - a)^2$ are added. Because order doesn't matter when adding integers, you know that the two expressions are equal.

38.

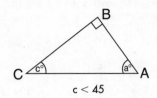

$c < 45$

Column A	Column B
The length of	The length of
$\overline{AB}$	$\overline{CB}$

39.

$$a > b + 1$$

Column A	Column B
a	b

38. Ⓐ Ⓑ Ⓒ Ⓓ

39. Ⓐ Ⓑ Ⓒ Ⓓ

Answer #38:   Ⓑ

Theorems: • If X and Y are the sides of a triangle, and x and y are the opposite angles, it follows that:
1) if $x > y$, then $X > Y$
2) if $X > Y$, then $x > y$
• The sum of the angles of a triangle is 180°

Concept: • Triangle geometry

The sum of the angle measures in a triangle is always 180°. Therefore, if you subtract the 90° indicated by the small square at vertex B, you are left with $a° + c° = 90°$.

In the problem definition you are told that $c < 45$. From this and the fact that $a + c = 90$, you can deduce that $a > 45$. Even though you don't know what a and c are, you can write their relationship as $a > 45 > c$.

Because angle A is greater than angle C, the side opposite angle A, $\overline{BC}$, is longer than the side opposite angle C, $\overline{AB}$. Hence, the value in Column B is greater than the value in Column A, and the correct answer is B.

Answer #39:   Ⓐ

Concept: • Inequalities

Problems like this occur on the SAT more to ensure that you are careful than to test some specific skill. The problem definition tells you that $a > b + 1$. You know that $b + 1 > b$, so you can write the relation between a and b as $a > b + 1 > b$.

Now you can read off the answer: The value in Column A, a, is greater than the value in Column B, b.

Note that if you were told $a < b + 1$, you couldn't ascertain the relationship between a and b because a might be a lot less than $b + 1$, in which case it would also be less than b, or it might be between b and $b + 1$, in which case $a > b$.

40.

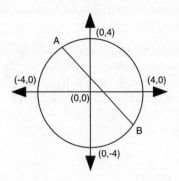

Column A	Column B
The length of $\overline{AB}$	8

40. Ⓐ   Ⓑ   Ⓒ   Ⓓ

Answer #40:   (B)

Theorem: • The diameter of the circle is the longest chord of the circle
Concept: • Circle geometry

$\overline{AB}$ is a chord of the circle but it's not the diameter, so its length must be less than the diameter of the circle. The diameter of the circle is the distance from (0,4) to (0, −4), which, by inspection, you can calculate to be 8. Therefore, AB is less than 8 and the value of Column A is less than the value of Column B.

SECTION 3

This section of the test requires you to enter your solution to each of the following ten problems onto a grid. The grid consists of four columns and twelve rows. To enter a number onto the grid, write each of its digits or symbols, in order, in the boxes at the top of the grid. Then, shade in the corresponding box beneath it. A decimal point is provided for numbers such as .5, and a slash is provided for constructing fractions such as $\frac{1}{2}$. The following are examples of correctly entered numbers:

Remember the following when entering numbers onto the grid:

- Mark no more than one box in any one column.

- No question will have a negative answer.

- If your answer is a *fraction*, remember to grid-in the fraction line in its own column.

- If your answer contains a *decimal point*, you must enter it, too, in its own column.

- *Mixed numbers,* such as $3\frac{1}{2}$, must be gridded-in using decimals (i.e., 3.5) or as improper fractions (i.e., $\frac{7}{2}$). If you enter your answer as a mixed number, it will be incorrect. In the case of $3\frac{1}{2}$, the machine scoring your test will interpret 31/2 as $\frac{31}{2} = 15.5$.

- If the answer to a problem is a repeating decimal, such as .3333 . . . (or $.\overline{3}$), you may round your solution to the most accurate answer the grid can accommodate (i.e., .333). Less accurate values, such as .3, are incorrect.

41. If $x = 2y = 4z$ and
$x + y + z = ay$, what is the
value of a?

42. A desk and chair set costs
$9.89. If a dozen sets are
purchased as a group, the
cost is reduced to $9.14 per
set. A school needs to buy
123 sets. How many dollars
does it save buying the sets
by the dozen instead of
individually?

41.

	/	/	
.	.	.	.
	0	0	0
1	1	1	1
2	2	2	2
3	3	3	3
4	4	4	4
5	5	5	5
6	6	6	6
7	7	7	7
8	8	8	8
9	9	9	9

42.

	/	/	
.	.	.	.
	0	0	0
1	1	1	1
2	2	2	2
3	3	3	3
4	4	4	4
5	5	5	5
6	6	6	6
7	7	7	7
8	8	8	8
9	9	9	9

Answer #41: 3.5 or $\dfrac{7}{2}$

Concept: • Solving equations

Looking at the right side of the second equation, ay, you can see that the important variable among x, y, and z is y. So, you'd like to rewrite the left side of that equation in terms of y. Using the first set of equations, you can replace every x in the second equation with $2y$. Likewise, you can replace every z in the second equation with $\dfrac{1}{2}y$. Doing these replacements in the second equation results in:

$$2y + y + \frac{1}{2}y = ay.$$

Now you can divide both sides of the equation by y to get

$$2 + 1 + \frac{1}{2} = a, \text{ or } 3\frac{1}{2} = a.$$

Warning: To grid in $3\dfrac{1}{2}$ you must write either "3.5" or "7/2." If you write "31/2" it will be misinterpreted as 15.5 and will be marked incorrect.*

Answer #42: 90

Concept: • Rates

For every set that the school buys as part of a dozen, it saves $\$9.89 - \$9.14 = \$.75$ per desk-and-chair set. However, if you were to multiply $\$.75$ by 123 sets, you'd be making a mistake. Remember that to receive the discounted price, the school must purchase 12 sets *as a group*. Ten groups of 12 sets is 120 sets; the last 3 sets must be purchased at the regular price. Therefore, the school saves:

$$.75\,\frac{\$}{\text{set}} \times 120 \text{ sets} = \$90.$$

Note that when you grid in the 90, you do not add the dollar sign.*

---

* Gridded-in answers to these problems appear on page 137.

43.

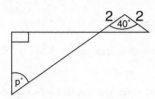

What is the value of p in the above figure?

44. If $(2^5 - 2^6)(2^0 - 2^1) = 2^x$, then what is the value of x?

43.

	/	/	
.	.	.	.
	0	0	0
1	1	1	1
2	2	2	2
3	3	3	3
4	4	4	4
5	5	5	5
6	6	6	6
7	7	7	7
8	8	8	8
9	9	9	9

44.

	/	/	
.	.	.	.
	0	0	0
1	1	1	1
2	2	2	2
3	3	3	3
4	4	4	4
5	5	5	5
6	6	6	6
7	7	7	7
8	8	8	8
9	9	9	9

Answer #43: 20

Theorems:
- In a triangle, angles opposite equal sides are equal
- Vertical angles are equal
- The sum of the angle measures in a triangle is 180°

Concept:
- Triangle geometry

By the time you have answered this problem, the diagram should be completely marked up. Start with it as it is presented and add information as you go. If you didn't mark up the figure, follow along now.

The unknown angles in the upper triangle are equal because they are opposite equal sides; draw an x in each one. Now you have three angles of a triangle, so their measures must sum to 180°. Write the equation $2x + 40 = 180$. Solving the equation for x you get $x = 70$. Replace the x's you wrote in with 70s. Because the two triangles share vertical angles and one of the angles is 70°, the other one must be, too. Write in 70° for the larger triangle's third angle measure. Now you have three angles listed for the larger triangle, 90°, 70°, and $p°$. They must sum to 180°, so you can set up the equation: $90 + 70 + p = 180$. Solving this equation, $p = 20$.*

Answer #44: 5

Formulas:
- $a^{x+y} = a^x a^y$
- If $a^x = a^y$, then $x = y$

Concepts:
- Exponents
- Arithmetic

With a fancier calculator you might be able to do this problem by brute force, calculating each of the values. A faster and less error-prone method is to factor the large exponents out of the expression $(2^5 - 2^6)$. The result of factoring 2^5 out of the first expression is:

$$2^5(2^0 - 2^1)(2^0 - 2^1).$$

Any number raised to the 0th power is 1, and any number raised to the 1st power is itself, so you can further simplify the given equation to be $2^5(1 - 2)(1 - 2) = 2^x$. The two $(1 - 2)$'s both simplify to -1, and when multiplied together yield 1; further simplifying, you are left with $2^5 = 2^x$, which implies $x = 5$.*

---

* Gridded-in answers to these problems appear on page 85.

45.

What is a possible value for the length of $\overline{AB}$?

46.

Test #	% Correct
1	90
2	75
3	95
4	90
5	85

This table shows the percentage of questions Lynn answered correctly on each of five 60-question tests. What was the total number of questions Lynn answered correctly on the five tests?

45.

	/	/	
.	.	.	.
	0	0	0
1	1	1	1
2	2	2	2
3	3	3	3
4	4	4	4
5	5	5	5
6	6	6	6
7	7	7	7
8	8	8	8
9	9	9	9

46.

	/	/	
.	.	.	.
	0	0	0
1	1	1	1
2	2	2	2
3	3	3	3
4	4	4	4
5	5	5	5
6	6	6	6
7	7	7	7
8	8	8	8
9	9	9	9

Answer #45:   Any number n such that $2 < n < 4$

Concept: • Coordinate geometry

Not all math problems have exact solutions. With the inclusion of "grid-in" problems on the SAT, it is possible for people to give different answers to a problem and all be correct.

     To solve this particular problem, notice that A lies somewhere between -2 and -1 and B is somewhere between 1 and 2. The operative word here is *somewhere*. To maximize the length of $\overline{AB}$ you can imagine A right up against the -2 and B up against the 2; in this case, the length of $\overline{AB}$ would be infinitesimally less than 4. To minimize the length of $\overline{AB}$ you can imagine A right up against the -1 and B right up against the 1; in this case, the length of $\overline{AB}$ is infinitesimally greater than 2. Any number between 2 and 4, therefore, is a correct answer; note that 2 and 4 are *not* correct answers.*

Answer #46:   261

Formula: • $a\%$ of $b = \dfrac{a}{100} \times b$

Concept: • Tables and graphs
                • Percentages

This is another problem where writing on the test can help you keep your numbers straight and avoid arithmetic errors. 90% of 60 is $\dfrac{9}{10} \times 60 = 9 \times 6 = 54$. Write 54 to the right of each of 90% in the table. Similarly, 75% of 60 is 45, 95% of 60 is 57, and 85% of 60 is 51. Again, write each of these values in the table. Now you have a third column with the number of questions Lynn answered correctly for each test. Summing 54, 45, 57, 54, and 51 gives you the answer 261.*

---

* Gridded-in answers to these problems appear on page 138.

47.
$$N = \{2, 4, 6\}$$
$$D = \{3, 6, 9\}$$

What is the positive square root of the difference between the greatest and least fractions that can be formed by choosing one number from set N to be the numerator and one number from set D to be the denominator?

48. It costs $18 to buy exactly enough paint to cover the surface of a solid cube. If the cube is spilt into two rectangular boxes, how much extra, in dollars, does it cost to paint the surfaces of the resulting two pieces?

47.

48.

Answer #47: $\dfrac{4}{3}$ or 1.33

Formula: • $\sqrt{\dfrac{a}{b}} = \dfrac{\sqrt{a}}{\sqrt{b}}$

Concepts: • Fractions
• Exponents and square roots

By taking the greatest numerator from set N and the least denominator from set D, you get the greatest possible fraction, $\dfrac{6}{3}$ = 2. Likewise, to generate the least possible fraction, take the least numerator from set N, 2, and the greatest denominator from set D, 9, to get $\dfrac{2}{9}$.

The problem asks for the square root of the difference between the two fractions. The difference between 2 and $\dfrac{2}{9}$ is $2 - \dfrac{2}{9} = \dfrac{18}{9} - \dfrac{2}{9} = \dfrac{16}{9}$. The square root of $\dfrac{16}{9}$ can be computed as follows:

$$\sqrt{\dfrac{16}{9}} = \dfrac{\sqrt{16}}{\sqrt{9}} = \pm\dfrac{4}{3}.$$

Since you're asked for the *positive* square root, pick $\dfrac{4}{3}$.*

Answer #48: 6

Formula: • A cube has six faces
Concepts: • Rectangle geometry
• Diagramming

Because a cube has six faces and it costs $18 to paint the cube, it must cost $3 to paint each face. When you split the cube into two rectangular boxes, you create two new faces. At $3 per face, the additional cost of paint is $6.*

If you're having a hard time visualizing this problem the following illustration may help.

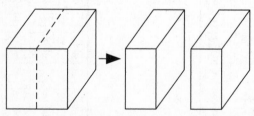

---

* Gridded-in answers to these problems appear on page 138.

49. A family consists of a pair of twin girls, age 6; a boy, age 10; and two parents, ages 38 and 40. What is the sum of the mean, the mode, and the median of their ages?

50.

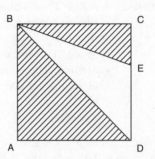

In this figure, ABCD is a square with area 2. If $\overline{DE}$ is twice as long as $\overline{EC}$, what is the area of $\triangle BED$?

49.

50.

Answer #49: 36

Definitions:
- Mean: This is another word for "average," this is the sum of the elements in a list divided by the number of elements in that list
- Mode: The element of a list that occurs most often
- Median: The element in a list for which half of the other elements are greater and the other half of the elements are less.

Concept:
- Averages

This problem is like a vocabulary quiz: if you know the definitions, you get the problem correct. The list of the family's ages, in ascending order, is {6, 6, 10, 38, 40}. The mode is the element that occurs the most often, 6. The median is the element in the middle. There are two ages greater than 10 and two less than 10, so 10 is the median. The mean is the sum of the ages divided by the number of ages. This comes out to:

$$\frac{6 + 6 + 10 + 38 + 40}{5} = \frac{100}{5} = 20.$$

So the sum of the mean, the mode, and the median of the family's ages is $6 + 10 + 20 = 36.$*

Answer #50: $\frac{2}{3}$ or .666 or .667

Formulas:
- Area of triangle $= \frac{1}{2} \times$ base $\times$ height
- Area of a square = length of a side squared

Concepts:
- Triangle geometry
- Rectangle geometry
- Diagramming

This problem states that ABCD has area 2. $\overline{BD}$ splits ABCD into 2 equal pieces, so ΔBCD has area 1. You are told that $\overline{ED}$ is twice as long as $\overline{CE}$, so add a point X that bisects $\overline{ED}$. Now you're left with three triangles: ΔBCE, ΔBEX, and ΔBXD.

Because of where you chose to place X, the lengths of their bases are equal. Furthermore, they all share the altitude $\overline{BC}$. So their areas must all be equal. Three equal triangles whose areas sum to 1 each have an area of $\frac{1}{3}$. The unshaded section of the square covers two of these triangles, so its area must be $\frac{2}{3}$.*

---

* Gridded-in answers to these problems appear on page 86.

This final section of Test 1 consists of ten problems, each of which has five possible answer choices. For each problem, select the answer choice that represents the best solution and shade the corresponding oval.

51. All of the following pairs (x, y) satisfy the inequality $y \leq x^2$ EXCEPT

(A) $(1, -2)$
(B) $(2, 4)$
(C) $(-2, 4)$
(D) $(-3, 4)$
(E) $(-1, 2)$

52. If $(3^2)(2^3) = 2(6^m)$, then $m =$

(A) 1
(B) 2
(C) 3
(D) 4
(E) 5

51. Ⓐ Ⓑ Ⓒ Ⓓ Ⓔ

52. Ⓐ Ⓑ Ⓒ Ⓓ Ⓔ

Answer #51:   (E)

Concept: • Arithmetic

There are no complicated skills being tested in this problem, just your ability to keep a lot of numbers organized. The correct solution is E, because −1 squared is 1 and 1 < 2. All of the other options satisfy the relation $y \le x^2$.

If you got this problem wrong, was it because you were working too fast? If so, slow down and pace yourself.

Answer #52:   (B)

Formula: • $a^n b^n = (ab)^n$

Concept: • Exponents

This is another problem that will take a relatively long time if you try to solve it by computing the values of all of the expressions but will go fairly quickly if you understand what's being tested. Instead of looking at the left side of the equation and immediately computing its value, step back and look for patterns.

There's a 2 on the right side of the equation, so first factor a 2 out of the left side to get: $(3^2)(2^2)2 = 2(6^m)$. Now you can divide both sides of the equation by 2, leaving you with $(3^2)(2^2) = 6^m$. Using the formula shown above, you can further simplify the left side of the equation to be $(3 \times 2)^2$ and rewrite the equation as $6^2 = 6^m$. Having done only minimal multiplication, you can arrive at the answer, $m = 2$.

53.

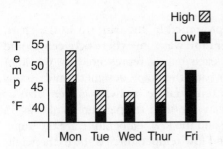

High and Low Temperatures for the Week

On which day of the week was the difference between the low and high temperatures the greatest?

(A) Monday
(B) Tuesday
(C) Wednesday
(D) Thursday
(E) Friday

54.

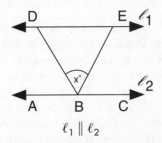

$\ell_1 \parallel \ell_2$

In the figure above, $\overline{BD}$ bisects $\angle ABE$ and $\overline{BE}$ bisects $\angle CBD$. What is the value of x?

(A) 30
(B) 45
(C) 60
(D) 90
(E) 120

53. Ⓐ Ⓑ Ⓒ Ⓓ Ⓔ

54. Ⓐ Ⓑ Ⓒ Ⓓ Ⓔ

Answer #53: (D)

Concept: • Tables and graphs

The low temperature for each day is represented by the dark bar in the chart. For example, on Monday, the low temperature was somewhere between 45 and 50 degrees. The high temperature for each day is represented by the light colored bar that sits on top of the darker bar—the graph designer could do this because she is guaranteed that the high temperature is always greater than or equal to the low temperature. On Monday the high temperature is almost 55 degrees. On Friday the high temperature and the low temperature are the same.

The difference between the high and low temperatures is the extra height added to each bar by the light colored section. By inspection, the bar with the largest light section is for Thursday, so the answer is (D).

If you were unsure whether the answer is Monday or Thursday, note that on Monday the light bar is less than the difference between 45 and 55—that is, less than 10. The light bar on Thursday is slightly greater than the difference between 45 and 55, that is, more than 10.

Answer #54: (C)

Concepts: • Triangle geometry
• Diagramming

When you're done working this problem, there should be three x's on the figure: the one originally there and two that you drew in. If you are going to perform well on the SAT, you *must* feel comfortable using and adding to the provided figures.

In this problem you're told that $\overline{BD}$ bisects $\angle ABE$. This means that the angles $\angle ABD$ and $\angle DBE$ have the same measure, $x°$. Similarly, because $\overline{BE}$ bisects $\angle CBD$, you can go through the same process and infer that $\angle CBE$ also has a measure of $x°$. Write these in.

Your diagram should now show a straight angle ($\angle ABC$) split into three equal parts. A straight angle has a measure of 180°, so each part must be 60°.

55. In a game of luck, there is a 1 in 10 chance of winning $10, a 1 in 5 chance of winning $5, and a 1 in 2 chance of winning $2. No other prizes are awarded, and a person cannot win more than one prize. What is the probability that a player will *not* win any money?

(A) 0
(B) .1
(C) .2
(D) .3
(E) 1

56.

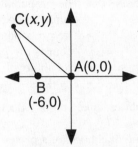

If the area of △ABC is 12, then the *y*-coordinate of *C* is:

(A) −4
(B)   4
(C) −2
(D)   2
(E) Cannot be determined from the information given

55. Ⓐ Ⓑ Ⓒ Ⓓ Ⓔ

56. Ⓐ Ⓑ Ⓒ Ⓓ Ⓔ

Answer #55: Ⓒ

Theorems:
- The probability that *either* of two independent, **exclusive** events will occur is the *sum* of their individual probabilities.
- The probability that *both* of two independent events will occur is the *product* of their individual probabilities.

Concepts:
- Probability
- Fractions

Probabilities, like ratios, decimals, and rates, involve computations with fractions.

The likelihood of a player winning a prize is either 1 in 10, 1 in 5, or 1 in 2. Written as fractions, these are $\frac{1}{10}$, $\frac{1}{5}$, and $\frac{1}{2}$. The probability that the player will win at least one of the prizes is the sum of the fractions:

$$\frac{1}{10} + \frac{1}{5} + \frac{1}{2} = \frac{8}{10} = \frac{4}{5}.$$

The probability that the player won't win any prize is the difference between 1 and the probability that the player will win a prize: $1 - \frac{4}{5} = \frac{1}{5}.$

Writing $\frac{1}{5}$ as a decimal yields .2, answer C.

Answer #56: Ⓑ

Formula:
- Area of a triangle $= \frac{1}{2} \times bh$

Concept:
- Coordinate geometry

You are given the area of $\triangle ABC$, so it's likely you'll need to use the formula for the area of a triangle to find the y-coordinate of C, which is also the height of the perpendicular line segment from C down to the x-axis. Draw this in. Notice that this is an altitude of $\triangle ABC$. Since the base of the triangle is 6, the length of $\overline{AB}$, you can plug into the formula:

$$\text{Area of } \triangle ABC = \frac{1}{2} \times \text{base} \times \text{height}$$

$$12 = \frac{1}{2} \times (6) \times (y)$$

$$4 = y$$

57. After the first two of four equal-length exams, Brenda had an 87% average. What is the least score Brenda can have on the third exam and still maintain at least a 90% average on all four tests?

(A) 83
(B) 86
(C) 87
(D) 93
(E) 96

58. A rhombus (a four-sided figure, all of whose sides are equal in length) has perimeter 20. If one of the diagonals has length 8, what is the length of the other diagonal?

(A) 3
(B) 5
(C) $5\sqrt{2}$
(D) 6
(E) 8

57. Ⓐ Ⓑ Ⓒ Ⓓ Ⓔ

58. Ⓐ Ⓑ Ⓒ Ⓓ Ⓔ

Answer #57: Ⓑ

Formula: • Average = $\dfrac{\text{sum of elements in a list}}{\text{number of elements in the list}}$

Concept: • Averages

Brenda received an average of 87% for the first two exams, so start by writing down: E_1: 87, E_2: 87. The problem is to find Brenda's score on the third exam, so write down E_3: x. Brenda wants to know how low she can score on the third exam and still be able to have a 90% average for the year; so, assume that she does the best she possibly can on the fourth exam, 100%. Now write down E_4: 100%.

   Plugging into the equation for computing an average:

$$90 = \frac{87 + 87 + x + 100}{4}$$

Solving for x step by step, you write:

$$90 = \frac{274 + x}{4}$$

$$360 = 274 + x$$

$$86 = x$$

If Brenda wants to average at least 90% on the four tests, she must get at least 86% on the third exam. If she gets less than 86% on this exam, there's nothing she can do on the final exam to get a 90% overall average.

Answer #58: Ⓓ

Formulas: • Pythagorean theorem: $x^2 + y^2 = z^2$
               • A common "Pythagorean triple" is: $3^2 + 4^2 = 5^2$

Concepts: • Triangle geometry
               • Diagramming

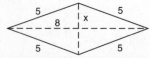

Start by drawing a picture. The figure has four equal sides. You know each side has a length of 5 because the perimeter is 20. The diagonal with the known length is marked with an 8; the other, unknown one with an x.

   Notice that the two diagonals bisect each other and form a 90° angle. Knowing this, add two 4s to your picture in place of the 8 and mark the angle between the diagonals as 90°. Taking a look at any one of the four triangles formed by the diagonals, you have a hypotenuse of 5 and a side of 4 in a right triangle. This is a Pythagorean triple! You should recognize that the unknown side is 3. The unknown side of the triangle is half of the diagonal you are looking for, so the length of the diagonal is 6, choice (D).

59. What is the least number
greater than 1 that has both
an integer square root and an
integer cube root?

(A) 8
(B) 16
(C) 27
(D) 64
(E) 81

60. Two buses travel the same
route. The first goes 55 miles
per hour, the second goes
65 mph. How much farther
has the faster bus driven
after $3\frac{1}{2}$ hours?

(A) 10 miles
(B) 35 miles
(C) 192.5 miles
(D) 227.5 minutes
(E) 300 miles

59. (A)   (B)   (C)   (D)   (E)

60. (A)   (B)   (C)   (D)   (E)

Answer #59:   (D)

Formulas:
- $2^0 = 1, 2^1 = 2, 2^2 = 4, \ldots 2^6 = 64$
- $1^2 = 1, 2^2 = 4, 3^2 = 9, \ldots 9^2 = 81$
- $1^3 = 1, 2^3 = 8, 3^3 = 27, 4^3 = 64$

Concepts:
- Exponents
- Factoring and prime factors

Exponents get very great, very quickly. Consequently, to test your knowledge of exponents, the SAT has to use small exponents or small bases. Because of this, it is worth your time to memorize the powers of 2 up to 2^6 and the perfect squares and cubes less than 100.

This problem asks you to find the least number, call it x, that has both a square root and a cube root. Going through the list of possible solutions:

8 is a perfect cube but not a square
16 is a perfect square but not a cube
27 is a perfect cube but not a square
64 is both a perfect square and a perfect cube
81 is a perfect square but not a cube

64 is the only possibility that is both a perfect square and a perfect cube, so the answer is (D).

Answer #60:   (B)

Formula:
- $\text{Rate} = \dfrac{\text{Amount}}{\text{Time}}$

Concept:
- Rates

I wanted to start this problem, "Two trains start in Chicago . . . ," but train problems are too clichéd for the SAT.

The simplest way to do this problem is to notice that the fast bus is going 10 mph faster than the slower bus. After $3\frac{1}{2}$ hours the faster bus has gone $3\frac{1}{2}$ hrs × 10 mph = 35 miles farther than the slow bus.

Another equally correct method of doing this problem is to figure out how far each bus went in $3\frac{1}{2}$ hours and then compute the difference. You should use the approach that takes you the least time and leaves you less prone to error.

Congratulations! You've now completed Test 1.

SOLUTIONS TO GRID-IN PROBLEMS

41.

	3	.	5
	/	/	
.	.	■	.
	0	0	0
1	1	1	1
2	2	2	2
3	■	3	3
4	4	4	4
5	5	5	■
6	6	6	6
7	7	7	7
8	8	8	8
9	9	9	9

42.

		9	0
	/	/	
.	.	.	.
	0	0	■
1	1	1	1
2	2	2	2
3	3	3	3
4	4	4	4
5	5	5	5
6	6	6	6
7	7	7	7
8	8	8	8
9	9	■	9

43.

		2	0
	/	/	
.	.	.	.
	0	0	■
1	1	1	1
2	2	■	2
3	3	3	3
4	4	4	4
5	5	5	5
6	6	6	6
7	7	7	7
8	8	8	8
9	9	9	9

44.

			5
	/	/	
.	.	.	.
	0	0	0
1	1	1	1
2	2	2	2
3	3	3	3
4	4	4	4
5	5	5	■
6	6	6	6
7	7	7	7
8	8	8	8
9	9	9	9

45.

			3
	/	/	
.	.	.	.
	0	0	0
1	1	1	1
2	2	2	2
3	3	3	■
4	4	4	4
5	5	5	5
6	6	6	6
7	7	7	7
8	8	8	8
9	9	9	9

46.

	2	6	1
	/	/	
.	.	.	.
	0	0	0
1	1	1	■
2	■	2	2
3	3	3	3
4	4	4	4
5	5	5	5
6	6	■	6
7	7	7	7
8	8	8	8
9	9	9	9

47.

	4	/	3
	/	■	
.	.	.	.
	0	0	0
1	1	1	1
2	2	2	2
3	3	3	■
4	■	4	4
5	5	5	5
6	6	6	6
7	7	7	7
8	8	8	8
9	9	9	9

48.

			6
	/	/	
.	.	.	.
	0	0	0
1	1	1	1
2	2	2	2
3	3	3	3
4	4	4	4
5	5	5	5
6	6	6	■
7	7	7	7
8	8	8	8
9	9	9	9

49.

		3	6
	/	/	
.	.	.	.
	0	0	0
1	1	1	1
2	2	2	2
3	3	■	3
4	4	4	4
5	5	5	5
6	6	6	■
7	7	7	7
8	8	8	8
9	9	9	9

50.

.	6	6	7
	/	/	
■	.	.	.
	0	0	0
1	1	1	1
2	2	2	2
3	3	3	3
4	4	4	4
5	5	5	5
6	■	■	6
7	7	7	■
8	8	8	8
9	9	9	9

This section consists of 60 problems and five possible answer choices for each. For each problem, select the answer choice that represents the best solution and shade the corresponding oval.

1. Brass pipe sells for $15 per foot. What is the cost of 4 yards of brass pipe?

   (A) $20
   (B) $42.50
   (C) $60
   (D) $97.50
   (E) $180

2. If $1.25\% = \dfrac{1}{x}$, then the value of x is

   (A) 0.8
   (B) 8
   (C) 80
   (D) 800
   (E) 8,000

1. Ⓐ Ⓑ Ⓒ Ⓓ Ⓔ

2. Ⓐ Ⓑ Ⓒ Ⓓ Ⓔ

Answer #1:   Ⓔ

Concept: • Converting units of measure
              • Formula 3 feet = 1 yard

First of all, we must determine the number of feet of pipe we are buying, if we're buying 4 yards of pipe.

   4 yards × 3 = 12 feet

   4 yards is 12 feet, and each foot of pipe costs $15.

   12 feet of pipe @ $15 a foot = 12 × $15 = $180

The total cost is $180.

Answer #2:   Ⓒ

Concept: • Renaming percents as fractions

It's easier to solve this particular question in two steps (renaming a percent as a decimal, then renaming the decimal as a fraction) than it is to do it in one step (renaming a percent as a fraction).

Let's rename the percent as a decimal:

   1.25% means 1.25 "per one hundred" or $\dfrac{1.25}{100}$.

   Divide 1.25 by 100 to get 0.0125.

Now let's rename the decimal as a fraction:

$$0.0125 = \frac{0125}{10,000} = \frac{125}{10,000}$$

Simplify the fraction (use small steps if you want to):

$$\frac{125}{10,000} = \frac{25}{2,000} = \frac{5}{400} = \frac{1}{80}$$

So 1.25% $= \dfrac{1}{80}$

3. If the pass rate of a certain exam is 93%, then how many of the 500 students who took the test failed it?

   (A) 7
   (B) 35
   (C) 93
   (D) 407
   (E) 465

4. If $4 - x \geq 3x + 5$, then

   (A) $x \leq -\dfrac{1}{4}$

   (B) $x \leq \dfrac{1}{4}$

   (C) $x \geq -\dfrac{1}{4}$

   (D) $x \geq \dfrac{1}{4}$

   (E) $x \geq \dfrac{3}{4}$

1. Ⓐ Ⓑ Ⓒ Ⓓ Ⓔ

2. Ⓐ Ⓑ Ⓒ Ⓓ Ⓔ

Answer #3:   Ⓑ

Concept: • Solving percent problems

Formula: • $percent = \dfrac{part}{whole}$

Be careful when answering this question. It gives you information about how many students *pass* a test, but then asks about how many students *fail* it. This is a perfect example of why you should read each test question very carefully before you start to calculate the answer.

There are two ways to calculate the answer to this question. Let's talk about them both.

We can multiply the 500 students who took the test by 93% (the percent who passed).

$$500 \times 93\% = 500 \times 0.93 = 465$$

(We're only half done, but notice that this trap answer is one of the choices.) 465 students passed, so how many failed? How many are left from the original 500 who took the test? $500 - 465$ failed.

$500 - 465 = 35$, so 35 students failed the test.

The other way to calculate the answer to this question is to work with the percents first. Since 93% passed, 100% − 93%, or 7%, failed. Now we multiply the 500 students who took the test by 7%.

$$500 \times 7\% = 500 \times 0.07 = 35$$

35 students failed the test.

Answer #4:   Ⓐ

Concept: • Solving inequalities

Solving inequalities is the same as solving regular equations, except that when you divide or multiply by a negative number you have to reverse the inequality sign.

Here's our inequality:

$$4 - x \geq 3x + 5$$

Subtract 4 from both sides to get

$$-x \geq 3x + 1$$

Subtract $3x$ from both sides to get

$$-4x \geq 1$$

Now divide both sides by −4. Don't forget to reverse the inequality sign.

$$x \leq -\frac{1}{4}$$

5. Which of the following expresses the distance 153,000,000 miles in scientific notation?

   (A) 1.53×10^6 miles
   (B) 15.3×10^6 miles
   (C) 1.53×10^7
   (D) 1.53×10^8
   (E) 15.3×10^8

6. $2\sqrt{8p^2k}(\sqrt{2k^3}) =$

   (A) $4pk^2$
   (B) $4p^2k^2$
   (C) $4\sqrt{2pk^2}$
   (D) $8pk^2$
   (E) $8p^2k^2$

1. (A) (B) (C) (D) (E)

2. (A) (B) (C) (D) (E)

Answer #5:   Ⓓ

Concept: • Scientific notation

The proper format for scientific notation is to move the decimal point so that there is only one digit to the left of the decimal point:

153,000,000.

1.53000000

Then count up the number of digits to the right of the decimal point (do this before you drop any extra zeros!).

There are 8 digits to the right of the decimal point, so multiply 1.53 by 10^8 (which is equal to 100,000,000). So

$$153,000,000 = 1.53 \times 10^8$$

Answer #6:   Ⓓ

Concept: • Properties of square roots

Formula: • $\sqrt{m} \times \sqrt{n} = \sqrt{mn}$

To solve this question, we need to combine first and then sort everything out.
First, multiply to combine:

$$2\sqrt{8p^2k} \times \sqrt{2k^3} = 2\sqrt{16p^2k^4}$$

Now, sort everything out:

The 2 stays outside the radical sign:

$$2\sqrt{16p^2k^4}$$

The square root of 16 is 4, so pull that out from under the radical sign:

$$2 \times 4\sqrt{p^2k^4}$$

The square root of p^2 is p, so pull that out from under the radical sign:

$$(2 \times 4)\,p\,\sqrt{k^4}$$

The square root of k^4 is k^2, so pull that out from under the radical sign:

$$(2 \times 4)\,pk^2$$

Now multiply the numbers:

$$8pk^2$$

7. What is the slope of a line that passes through the points $(5, -2)$ and $(-1, 3)$?

(A) $-\dfrac{5}{6}$

(B) $-\dfrac{6}{5}$

(C) $-\dfrac{3}{2}$

(D) $\dfrac{5}{6}$

(E) $\dfrac{3}{2}$

8. A large drink and a small drink together cost $8.00. If the large drink costs $1.60 more than the small drink does, what is the price of the small drink?

(A) $1.60
(B) $2.40
(C) $3.20
(D) $3.40
(E) $4.80

1. Ⓐ Ⓑ Ⓒ Ⓓ Ⓔ

2. Ⓐ Ⓑ Ⓒ Ⓓ Ⓔ

Answer #7: Ⓐ

Concept: • Slope of a line

Formula: • Slope $= \dfrac{y_2 - y_1}{x_2 - x_1}$

Slope questions can occasionally be tricky, but this one is very straightforward. Just plug the numbers into the slope formula, and you're done. Don't overthink it.

y_2 is the y coordinate from the second coordinate pair.
y_1 is the y coordinate from the first coordinate pair.
x_2 is the x coordinate from the second coordinate pair.
x_2 is the x coordinate from the first coordinate pair.

$$\frac{3 - -2}{-1 - 5} = \frac{5}{-6} = -\frac{5}{6}$$

(Even if you can't remember the slope formula, you can still draw a rough sketch of where these points would lie on a coordinate plane to figure out that the slope would be negative. Then you could have a 33% chance of guessing the right answer from among the negative answers.)

Answer #8: Ⓒ

Concept: • Solving algebraic word problems with two unknowns

There are two ways to solve this problem. Let's use algebra first.

Let $x =$ the unknown quantity we're looking for, and then we'll express the other unknown in terms of x.

x is the price of the small drink. This means that $x + \$1.60$ is the price of the large drink. Since the cost of the two drinks together is $8.00, we can set up the equation

$$x + (x + \$1.60) = \$8.00$$

Now solve for x.

$$2x + \$1.60 = \$8.00$$
$$2x = \$6.40$$
$$x = \$3.20$$

The other way to solve the problem is to walk through it logically, without using algebra. Since the only difference between the prices of the two drinks is $1.60, if we remove the $1.60 from the equation, the prices would theoretically be the same.

$$\$8.00 - \$1.60 = \$6.40$$

Now divide the $6.40 by 2 (for the 2 drinks):

$$\$6.40 \div 2 = \$3.20$$

$3.20 is the price of the small drink. ($3.20 + $1.60, or $4.80, is the price of the large drink, but the question doesn't ask us about that.)

9. If $\dfrac{5y + 3}{3} = 4y - 1$, what is the value of y?

(A) $\dfrac{6}{7}$

(B) $\dfrac{7}{6}$

(C) $-\dfrac{4}{7}$

(D) $-\dfrac{6}{7}$

(E) $-\dfrac{7}{6}$

10. If a car is traveling at a speed of 30 miles per hour, how many minutes will it take the car to travel 5 miles?

(A) 8
(B) 10
(C) 12
(D) 15
(E) 18

1. Ⓐ Ⓑ Ⓒ Ⓓ Ⓔ

2. Ⓐ Ⓑ Ⓒ Ⓓ Ⓔ

Answer #9: Ⓐ

Concept: • Solving equations

The key to solving this question is approaching the equation in small steps. First, let's multiply both sides by 3:

$$5y + 3 = 12y - 3$$

Now let's subtract $5y$ from both sides:

$$3 = 7y - 3$$

Then add 3 to both sides:

$$6 = 7y$$

Finally, let's divide both sides by 7:

$$\frac{6}{7} = y$$

Answer #10: Ⓑ

Concept: • Converting units of measure

Formula: • 60 minutes = 1 hour

The car goes 30 miles every hour. How long will it take the car to go 5 miles? In other words, what part of 30 is 5?

$$\frac{5}{30} = \frac{1}{6}$$

5 is $\frac{1}{6}$ of 30. So it will take the car $\frac{1}{6}$ of 60 minutes to go 5 miles.

$$\frac{1}{6} \times 60 = \frac{60}{6} = 10$$

It will take the car 10 minutes to go 5 miles.

11. The greatest prime factor of 242 is

(A) 2
(B) 3
(C) 6
(D) 11
(E) 22

12. If $|x + 5 - 2x| = 6$, then x must be

(A) greater than 10
(B) less than 0
(C) between 0 and 10
(D) between -2 and 12
(E) between 0 and 12

---

1. (A) (B) (C) (D) (E)

2. (A) (B) (C) (D) (E)

Answer #11: Ⓓ

Definition: • Greatest prime factor

To understand what "greatest prime factor" means, let's break it down into its parts. A factor is a number that divides another number. For instance, 2 and 3 are some factors of 6. A prime number is a number that has exactly two factors, namely itself and 1. And "greatest" means that we're looking for the greatest of the available numbers.

Let's take a look at the question itself. Since we're trying to find the greatest prime factor, we're looking for the greatest possible number that divides 242 and is also prime. Therefore, it makes the most sense to start trying out the greatest numbers first.

We can start with choice (E), 22. However, 22 is not a prime number. So let's eliminate it and go on to the next greatest choice, (D), 11. 11 is a prime number. Is 242 divisible by 11? Yes. $242 \div 11 = 22$. The answer is (D).

If you want to make sure, you can check the other answer choices. Eliminate (C), 6, because it is not a prime number (242 is also not divisible by 6). Eliminate (B), 3, because 242 is not divisible by 3. Choice (A), 2, is prime, and 242 is divisible by 2. This means that 2 is a prime factor of 242, but it is not the greatest prime factor. So the answer is still (D).

Answer #12: Ⓓ

Definition: • Absolute value

Concept: • Solving an equation containing an absolute value

Absolute value means that you only take the positive value of whatever's between the | | lines. What that means, though, is that you have to take both solutions—positive and negative—into account when solving. In other words, we'll solve to make the equation equal to both 6 and -6, since the | | lines means that we can ignore the negative sign. Let's find both solutions, starting with the positive solution: $x + 5 - 2x = 6$

Combine the x values:	$5 - x =$	6
Subtract 5 from both sides:	$-x =$	1
Divide each side by -1:	$x =$	-1

This means that one value of x is -1. Before we find the other solution, let's look at the answer choices and see if we can eliminate anything. Eliminate choice (A), because -1 is not greater than 10. Eliminate choice (C), because -1 is not between 0 and 10. Eliminate choice (E), because -1 is not between 0 and 12. Now let's find the negative solution: $x + 5 - 2x = -6$

Combine the x values:	$5 - x =$	-6
Subtract 5 from both sides:	$-x =$	-11
Divide each side by -1:	$x =$	11

The other value of x is 11. We can eliminate choice (B), because 11 is not less than 0. The only answer that works is choice (D), because -1 and 11 (our two values of x) are between -2 and 12.

13. 9 is one-third percent of what number?

    (A) 0.27
    (B) 2.7
    (C) 27
    (D) 270
    (E) 2,700

14. The number 64,325.7, when rounded to the nearest ten, is

    (A) 64,325
    (B) 63,326
    (C) 64,320
    (D) 64,330
    (E) 64,400

1. Ⓐ Ⓑ Ⓒ Ⓓ Ⓔ

2. Ⓐ Ⓑ Ⓒ Ⓓ Ⓔ

Answer #13:   Ⓔ

Concept: • Expressing percents as decimals

Formula: • $A\% = \dfrac{A}{100}$

If 9 is $\dfrac{1}{3}$%, then multiply by 3 to find 1%. 27 is 1%. Since 1% really means $\dfrac{1}{100}$, set up a proportion:

$$\frac{1}{100} = \frac{27}{x}$$

x is the number we don't know. Now we can cross-multiply:

$1x = 27 \times 100$, or $x = 2{,}700$

Answer #14:   Ⓓ

Concept: • Rounding whole numbers

Let's review the names of the places:

    6 = ten thousand
    4 = thousand
    3 = hundred
    2 = ten
    5 = unit (or "one")
    7 = tenth

Since we're rounding this number to the nearest ten, we need to look at the value of the units digit (or "ones" digit). It's 5, so that means we round the tens digit up to 3. (Anything below 5 gets rounded down, while 5 or higher gets rounded up.) So the answer is 64,330.

15. A square with a perimeter of 20 has the same area as a triangle with a height of 5 and a base of

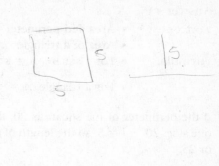

(A) 2.5
(B) 5
(C) 10
(D) 20
(E) 25

---

15. Ⓐ Ⓑ Ⓒ Ⓓ Ⓔ

Answer #15: Ⓒ

Concept: • Area and perimeter of a square
            • Area of a triangle

Formula: • For a square, $A = s^2$ and $P = 4s$

            • For a triangle, $A = \frac{1}{2}bb$

If the perimeter of the square is 20, then divide that by 4 to find the length of one side. $20 \div 4 = 5$, so the length of a side is 5. The area of the square is 5×5, or 25.

Now we know that the area of the triangle is also 25. Since the height of the triangle is 5, let's put the numbers we have into the formula for the area of a triangle:

$$25 = \frac{1}{2}5b, \text{ or } 25 = \frac{5b}{2}$$

Multiply both sides by 2: $50 = 5b$
and divide both sides by 5: $10 = b$

The base of the triangle is 10.

16. If $(4 - x)^3 > (4 + x)^3$, which of the following could be the value of x?

(A) -6
(B) 0
(C) $\dfrac{1}{2}$
(D) 1
(E) 10

---

16. Ⓐ Ⓑ Ⓒ Ⓓ Ⓔ

Answer #16: Ⓐ

Concepts: • Trinomial products
                • Inequalities and exponents

There are a few ways to solve this problem. The first way is to determine that, because each equation is raised to the power of 3, it will retain its own positive or negative status. The equation is saying, essentially, that the left side is greater than the right side. The only way that could happen is if a) both of the equations turned into fractions between 0 and 1 (because those get lesser the greater the exponent is), or b) the left equation will become positive and the right equation negative. Since both of these equations can't become fractions between 0 and 1, it has to be that the left one is positive and the right one's negative. What *that* means is that x has to be a negative number with an absolute value greater than 4. The only answer choice that fits is (A), -6. Notice that the question isn't asking you what the only possible value of x is, just which of the available numbers in the answer choices could be x.

Now, if you're completely confused by the paragraph above, there's still a great way for you to solve this problem: stick the answer choices, one by one, into the equation and see which one works. You can go in any order you want to, although it would probably be easiest to start with 0 or 1, since the math will be easier. But, for the sake of this explanation, let's go in the order they're given.

$$(4 - -6)^3 = (4 + 6)^3 = (10)^3 = 1000 \qquad (4 - 6)^3 = (-2)^3 = -8$$

1,000 is greater than -8, so the correct answer is (A). Let's check the other answer choices.

$$(4 - 0)^3 = (4)^3 = 64 \qquad (4 + 0)^3 = (4)^3 = 64$$

These are equal. Eliminate choice (B).

$$\left(4 - \frac{1}{2}\right)^3 = \left(\frac{7}{2}\right)^3 = \frac{7^3}{2^3} \qquad \left(4 + \frac{1}{2}\right)^3 = \left(\frac{9}{2}\right)^3 = \frac{9^3}{2^3}$$

The right side is greater than the left side. Eliminate choice (C).

$$(4 - 1)^3 = (3)^3 = 27 \qquad (4 + 1)^3 = (5)^3 = 125$$

The right side is greater than the left side. Eliminate choice (D).

$$(4 - 10)^3 = (-6)^3 = -216 \qquad (4 + 10)^3 = (14)^3 = 14^3$$

Since the right side is positive, the right side is greater than the left. Eliminate choice (E).

17.

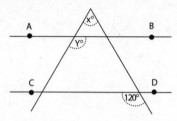

If $\overline{AB}$ is parallel to $\overline{CD}$ and $x = 60$, then what is the value of y?

(A) 180
(B) 120
(C) 90
(D) 60
(E) 45

18. What is the value of $\frac{2}{5}$ of 5 percent of 10?

(A) 0.2
(B) 0.4
(C) 1.0
(D) 2.0
(E) 2.5

1. Ⓐ Ⓑ Ⓒ Ⓓ Ⓔ

2. Ⓐ Ⓑ Ⓒ Ⓓ Ⓔ

Answer #17: (B)

Concepts:
- Vertical angles, alternate interior angles
- Equilateral triangles
- Parallel lines
- Degrees in a line

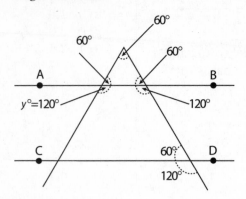

There are 180° in a line, so the angle that forms a line with the 120° angle must be 60°. Since $\overline{AB}$ and $\overline{CD}$ are parallel and x is 60, you know that both the triangles (the small one formed by $\overline{AB}$ and the big one formed by $\overline{CD}$) are equilateral triangles, so all the angles are 60°. Since there are 180° in a straight line, the measure of y must be 120°.

Answer #18: (A)

Concept:
- Fraction-decimal-percent equations

When you see the word "of" in a word problem, it means "multiplied by." So in this case, $\frac{2}{5}$ of 5 percent of 10 means

$$\frac{2}{5} \times .05 \times 10$$

Multiply through to get

$$\frac{2 \times .05 \times 10}{5} = \frac{1}{5}$$

Now divide 1 by 5 to get the decimal equivalent of the fraction

$$5\overline{)1}^{\,.2}$$

19. If $5x = \dfrac{3}{2}y$, then what is the value of $\dfrac{y}{\dfrac{10}{3}x}$?

(A) $\dfrac{10}{3}$

(B) 2

(C) $\dfrac{3}{2}$

(D) $\dfrac{2}{3}$

(E) 1

1. (A) (B) (C) (D) (E)

Answer #19: Ⓔ

Concept: • Equations with 2 variables

You can solve this problem a few ways. The first way is to solve for y.

$$5x = \frac{3}{2}y$$

Multiply both sides by 2.　　$10x = 3y$

　Divide both sides by 3.　　$\frac{10}{3}x = y$

Now put in $\frac{10}{3}x$ when you see y.　　$\dfrac{y}{\frac{10}{3}x} = \dfrac{\frac{10}{3}x}{\frac{10}{3}x} = 1$

The other way to solve this problem is to pick a number to put in for x, then solve the equation for y, and then put those numbers into the statement.

Let's make $x = 2$.　　$5 \times 2 = \frac{3}{2}y$, so $10 = \frac{3}{2}y$

Multiply both sides by 2.　　$20 = 3y$

Divide both sides by 3.　　$\frac{20}{3} = y$

So if $x = 2$, then $y = \frac{20}{3}$.

Now put those values into the statement $\dfrac{y}{\frac{10}{3}x}$.

$$\dfrac{\frac{20}{3}}{\frac{10}{3} \times 2} = \dfrac{\frac{20}{3}}{\frac{20}{3}} = 1$$

Either way you solve it, the answer is 1.

20. Square A has an area exactly four times that of Square B. The length of a side of Square A is decreased by 10%, and the length of a side of Square B is increased by 10%. Which of the following is closest to the ratio of the area of Square A to the area of Square B?

(A) 5:1
(B) 4:1
(C) 3:1
(D) 1:1
(E) 1:3

1. (A) (B) (C) (D) (E)

Answer #20: Ⓒ

Concepts:
- Area of squares
- Ratios
- Percents

Let's approach this question by picking some hypothetical numbers to work with. Let's make the area of Square A 400 and the area of Square B 100. That makes each side of Square A equal to 20, and each side of Square B equal to 10.

Now let's decrease the side of Square A by 10%.

$$20 \times 0.10 = 2$$

Subtract 2 from 20, and the new side is 18. Now the area of Square A is 18 by 18, or 324.

Now let's increase the side of Square B by 10%.

$$10 \times 0.10 = 1$$

Add 1 to 10, and the new side is 11. Now the area of Square B is 11 by 11, or 121.

The ratio of the area of Square A to the area of Square B is 324 to 121. Of the available answer choices, this is closest to 3:1.

(You could also answer this question algebraically, but it's a huge pain in the neck. Make the area of Square A equal to $4x$, and the area of Square B equal to x. That means the side of Square A is $\sqrt{4x}$, or $2\sqrt{x}$. Decreasing that by 10% would mean determining what 10% of $2\sqrt{x}$ is and then subtracting that from $2\sqrt{x}$. It's probably easier to use fractions to do that than it is to use decimals. Then you repeat the process with Square B, but you increase the side by 10%. At this point you'd probably just give up and think of some hypothetical numbers to use to get through the problem. Good instinct.)

21. If P is an integer that is divisible by 9 but not by 6, which of the following cannot be an integer?

(A) $\dfrac{P}{27}$

(B) $\dfrac{P}{3}$

(C) $\dfrac{P}{2}$

(D) $\dfrac{P}{1}$

(E) $\dfrac{\frac{P}{3}}{2}$

---

1. Ⓐ Ⓑ Ⓒ Ⓓ Ⓔ

Answer #21: Ⓒ

Concept: • Rules of divisibility
Definitions: • Divisible, integer

The easiest way to solve this problem is to pick numbers that are divisible by 9 but not by 6, and then put them into the answer choices to try to find the one that can't be an integer. Let's make it easy and start with 9 (which, of course, is divisible by 9 but not by 6).

$\dfrac{9}{27} = \dfrac{1}{3}$, which is not an integer, so leave choice (A) in.

$\dfrac{9}{3} = 3$, which is an integer, so eliminate choice (B).

$\dfrac{9}{2}$ is not an integer, so leave choice (C) in.

$\dfrac{9}{1} = 9$, which is an integer, so eliminate choice (D).

$\dfrac{9}{\frac{3}{2}} = 9 \times \dfrac{2}{3} = \dfrac{18}{3} = 6$, which is an integer, so eliminate choice (E).

You're left with (A) and (C). Try another number that is divisible by 9 but not by 6. How about 27?

$\dfrac{27}{27} = 1$, which is an integer, so eliminate choice (A).

$\dfrac{27}{2}$ is not an integer, so the correct answer is (C).

The other, more theoretical way to answer the question is to determine that if a number is divisible by 9 (which is 3 times 3) but not by 6 (which is 3 times 2), it must not be divisible by 2. Therefore, $\dfrac{P}{2}$ will not be an integer.

22. Which of the following is equal to the value of $\dfrac{\cos 45°}{\sin 45°}$?

    (A) tan 1°

    (B) tan 45°

    (C) sin 30°

    (D) cos 30°

    (E) It cannot be determined from the information given.

2. (A) (B) (C) (D) (E)

Answer #22: (B)

Concept:	• Trigonometric functions
Definitions:	• Sine, cosine, tangent

You won't be expected to know most of the sines, cosines, and tangents off the top of your head, but you should definitely know the values for isosceles right triangles and 30-60-90 triangles. Since $\cos 45° = 2\sqrt{2}$, as does $\sin 45°$, the value of $\dfrac{\cos 45°}{\sin 45°}$ is $\dfrac{2\sqrt{2}}{2\sqrt{2}}$, or 1. Since you can calculate a value, eliminate choice (E) right away.

Choice (A) is there to distract you, in case you make a mistake and think that tan 1° is equal to 1. The value of tan 45° is 1, so the correct answer is (B).

If your first instinct was to think that the value of $\dfrac{\cos 45°}{\sin 45°}$ must be cot 45° (because $\dfrac{\cos}{\sin}$ always equals cot), good! It's true that tan 45° is equal to cot 45°.

23. If the average cost of six paintings is $52,000, and the average cost of the two most expensive of those paintings is $71,000, what is the average cost of the remaining four paintings?

   (A) $19,000
   (B) $29,000
   (C) $42,500
   (D) $49,500
   (E) $60,250

24.

On the number line above, what value corresponds to the point that is $\frac{3}{5}$ of the distance from A to B?

   (A) 2.69
   (B) 2.76
   (C) 2.80
   (D) 2.85
   (E) 3.11

1. Ⓐ Ⓑ Ⓒ Ⓓ Ⓔ

2. Ⓐ Ⓑ Ⓒ Ⓓ Ⓔ

Answer #23: Ⓒ

Concept: • Averages

There are three parts to an average equation:

$$\frac{Total}{Number} = Average$$

The average of six paintings is $52,000.

$$\frac{Total}{6} = 52{,}000, \text{ so the total is } \$312{,}000.$$

If the two most expensive of those paintings average $71,000, then

$$\frac{Total}{2} = 71{,}000 \text{ and the total for the two paintings is } \$142{,}000.$$

Subtract the total of the expensive paintings from the total of all the paintings.

$$\$312{,}000 - \$142{,}000 = \$170{,}000.$$

The total of the remaining four paintings is $170,000.

$$\frac{170{,}000}{4} = 42{,}500$$

Answer #24: Ⓑ

Concepts: • Number line
                  • Fraction-decimal equivalents

According to the number line, point A is at 2.55 and point B is at 2.90. Therefore, the distance from A to B is 2.90 − 2.55, or 0.35.

Now let's determine what $\frac{3}{5}$ of 0.35 is.

$$\frac{3}{5} \times 0.35 = \frac{3 \times 0.35}{5} = \frac{3 \times 0.07}{1} = 0.21$$

So 0.21 is $\frac{3}{5}$ of 0.35. We're looking for the value on the number line, though. So add 0.21 to the value of point A (2.55) to get 2.76.

25. What is the distance between the points with coordinates $(-3,2)$ and $(2,-3)$?

(A) $2\sqrt{5}$

(B) $\sqrt{25}$

(C) $5\sqrt{2}$

(D) $\sqrt{61}$

(E) $6\sqrt{2}$

1. Ⓐ Ⓑ Ⓒ Ⓓ Ⓔ

Answer #25: Ⓒ

Concept: • Finding the distance between two points

Formula: • The distance formula $\sqrt{(x_2 - x_1)^2 + (y_2 - y_1)^2} = d$

There are two ways to solve this problem. The first way is to realize that you can find the distance between any two points on the coordinate plane by adding a third imaginary point to make a right triangle and using the Pythagorean Theorem to find the distance between the points. We can do that here by drawing a rough sketch:

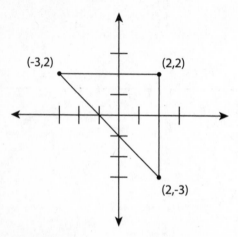

Here we've plotted the points and added the point (2,2) to make a right triangle. The two legs of the triangle are 5 and 5, and the hypotenuse is the distance we're looking for.

You may have the side ratios for isosceles right triangles memorized (a, a, $a\sqrt{2}$). If not, we can use the Pythagorean Theorem to find the hypotenuse:

$$5^2 + 5^2 = 25 + 25 = 50$$

The square root of 50 is $\sqrt{50} = \sqrt{25 \times 2} = 5\sqrt{2}$.

Of course, you can also just plug the coordinates into the distance formula.

$$\sqrt{(x_2 - x_1)^2 + (y_2 - y_1)^2} = d$$

$$\sqrt{(2 - -3)^2 + (-3 - 2)^2} = \sqrt{(5)^2 + (-5)^2}$$

$$= \sqrt{25 + 25}$$

$$= \sqrt{50}$$

$$= \sqrt{25 \times 2}$$

$$= 5\sqrt{2}$$

26. If $x + \dfrac{x}{2} + \dfrac{x}{3} + \dfrac{x}{4} = 75$, then what is the value of x?

(A) 3
(B) 9
(C) 12
(D) 22
(E) 36

---

1. Ⓐ Ⓑ Ⓒ Ⓓ Ⓔ

Answer #26: (E)

Concepts:
- Solving equations with one variable
- Adding fractions
- Common denominators

The easiest way to solve this problem is to find a common denominator to get rid of the fractions. If we multiply both sides of the equation by 12, we will eliminate the fractions and our addition will be much simpler.

$$12x + \frac{12x}{2} + \frac{12x}{3} + \frac{12x}{4} = 75 \times 12, \text{ becomes}$$

$$12x + 6x + 4x + 3x = 75(12), \text{ or } 25x = 75(12).$$

Now divide both sides by 25.

$$x = 3(12) = 36$$

27. On Saturday, a vendor sold $\frac{4}{9}$ of her original inventory. On Sunday, the vendor sold $\frac{3}{5}$ of her remaining inventory. What fraction of her original inventory does she have left?

(A) $-\frac{2}{45}$

(B) $\frac{2}{5}$

(C) $\frac{2}{9}$

(D) $\frac{2}{15}$

(E) $\frac{2}{45}$

28. A wall is 18 feet high and 90 feet long. If one gallon of paint covers 80 square feet of wall, what is the least number of gallons the painters will need to ensure that they can cover the entire wall with paint?

(A) 18
(B) 19
(C) 20
(D) 21
(E) 22

1. Ⓐ Ⓑ Ⓒ Ⓓ Ⓔ

2. Ⓐ Ⓑ Ⓒ Ⓓ Ⓔ

Answer #27: Ⓒ

Concepts: • Multiplying fractions
   • Solving for an unknown

You can solve this problem two ways. The first way is by multiplying the fractions. She sold $\frac{4}{9}$ the first day, so she had $\frac{5}{9}$ left. The second day she sold $\frac{3}{5}$ of the $\frac{5}{9}$ that was left. Multiply $\frac{5}{9}$ by $\frac{3}{5}$ to find out what fraction that was.

$$\frac{5}{9} \times \frac{3}{5} = \frac{15}{45} = \frac{1}{3}$$

She sold $\frac{1}{3}$ of the original inventory on Sunday.

She sold $\frac{4}{9}$ on Saturday and $\frac{1}{3}$ on Sunday, so she sold $\frac{4}{9} + \frac{1}{3} = \frac{4}{9} + \frac{3}{9} = \frac{7}{9}$ total. This means she has $\frac{2}{9}$ left.

The other way to solve the problem is to just pick a number to stand in for the inventory she started with. You want something divisible by 9 and by 5, so try 45. If she sold $\frac{4}{9}$ of that 45 the first day, this means she sold 20 (because $\frac{4}{9} \times 45$ $= \frac{4 \times 5}{1} = 20$) and had 25 left. If she sold $\frac{3}{5}$ of the remaining 25 on Sunday, that means she sold 15 (because $\frac{3}{5} \times 25 = \frac{3 \times 5}{1} = 15$). She sold 20 + 15, or 35, over the two days, so she has 10 left. 10 of the original 45 is $\frac{10}{45}$, or $\frac{2}{9}$.

Answer #28: Ⓓ

Concept: • Area of a rectangle

If the wall is 18 feet by 90 feet, the total area is 18 × 90 = 1,620 square feet. Since each gallon of paint covers 80 square feet, we need to divide 1,620 by 80 to figure out how many gallons of paint we need.

$$1{,}620 \div 80 = 80\overline{)1620} = 80\overline{)1620.00}^{\,20.25}$$

So 20.25 gallons of paint will cover the wall. We can only buy whole gallons of paint, though, so we need to buy 21 gallons total.

29. The number 46 is what percent of 1,000?

(A) 46%
(B) 4.6%
(C) 0.46%
(D) 0.046%
(E) 0.0046%

30. A certain cut of beef always loses 12% of its weight during the cooking process. If the cooked weight of a beef portion needs to be 6.6 ounces, what is the required weight of the portion before the cooking process?

(A) 8.0 ounces
(B) 7.5 ounces
(C) 7.4 ounces
(D) 7.2 ounces
(E) 6.8 ounces

1. Ⓐ Ⓑ Ⓒ Ⓓ Ⓔ

2. Ⓐ Ⓑ Ⓒ Ⓓ Ⓔ

Answer #29: Ⓑ

Concept: • Percent-fraction-decimal conversions

This has the potential to be a tricky question if you think too hard about it. Instead, use small steps. Start by renaming the numbers as a fraction:

46 of 1,000 is $\dfrac{46}{1,000}$.

Divide to get the decimal. $1,000\overline{)46.000}$ with quotient 0.046

Now, since "percent" really means "per one hundred", move the decimal point two spaces to the right to get the number expressed as a percent.

$0.046 = 4.6\%$

Answer #30: Ⓑ

Concept: • Percents

Essentially, what this question is asking is "6.6 is equal to what number minus 12% of that number?"

Writing that as an equation we get $6.6 = x - (0.12x)$

Let's simplify. $6.6 = 0.88x$

Now divide both sides by 0.88. $0.88\overline{)6.6}$ with quotient 7.5

The answer is 7.5.

Of course, the math is much easier if you just try out some of the answer choices. Let's start with (C), so we'll know if we're too high or too low if (C) isn't the answer.

7.4 is the starting weight, so let's calculate 12% of 7.4.

$7.4 \times 0.12 = 0.888$

Now subtract 0.888 from 7.4. $7.4 - 0.888 = 6.512$

Close, but not exactly. Eliminate (C). And eliminate (D) and (E), too, because they must also be too small. Try (B).

Calculate 12% of 7.5.

$7.5 \times 0.12 = 0.9$

Now subtract 0.9 from 7.5.

$7.5 - 0.9 = 6.6$

The answer is (B).

31. $(\cot\alpha \cdot \cos\alpha + \sin\alpha) \sin\alpha =$

(A) 0
(B) $\sin\alpha$
(C) $\cos\alpha$
(D) $\tan\alpha$
(E) 1

32. Dan can upholster 150 ottomans in 50 days. How many ottomans can he upholster in 30 days?

(A) 10
(B) 30
(C) 90
(D) 150
(E) 450

31. Ⓐ Ⓑ Ⓒ Ⓓ Ⓔ

32. Ⓐ Ⓑ Ⓒ Ⓓ Ⓔ

Answer #31: (E)

Concept: • Simplifying trigonometric expressions

Formulas: • $\cos^2\alpha + \sin^2\alpha = 1$

• $\cot\alpha = \dfrac{\cos\alpha}{\sin\alpha}$

To break down this equation, let's rewrite everything in terms of sines and cosines.

$$\left(\frac{\cos\alpha}{\sin\alpha}\cdot\cos\alpha + \sin\alpha\right)\sin\alpha$$

Now multiply inside the parentheses.

$$\left(\frac{\cos^2\alpha}{\sin\alpha} + \sin\alpha\right)\sin\alpha$$

Now multiply by what's outside the parentheses.

$$\left(\frac{\cos^2\alpha\cdot\sin\alpha}{\sin\alpha} + \sin^2\alpha\right)$$

Then divide.

$$\cos^2\alpha + \sin^2\alpha$$

The value of this expression, $\cos^2\alpha + \sin^2\alpha$, is 1.

Answer #32: (C)

Concepts: • Solving proportion problems
              • Solving rate problems

Formula: • If $\dfrac{a}{b} = \dfrac{c}{d}$, then $ad = bc$

This problem can be solved either as a proportion problem or as a rate problem.

To solve it as a proportion problem, just set up your proportion, using x to be the number of ottomans he can upholster in 30 days.

$$\frac{150\text{ ottomans}}{50\text{ days}} = \frac{x\text{ ottomans}}{30\text{ days}}$$

Cross-multiply. $150\cdot 30 = 50x$

$$4500 = 50x$$

Divide both sides by 50. $90 = x$

To solve this as a rate problem, figure out how many ottomans Dan can upholster in one day. If he does 150 in 50 days, divide 150 by 50.

$$50\overline{)150}\quad\overset{3}{}$$

He upholsters 3 ottomans each day. To determine how many he can upholster in 30 days, multiply 30 days by 3 per day.

$$30\cdot 3 = 90$$

33. Last year, the school fund-raiser made $2,120 for the school. This year, the fundraiser only made $1,802 for the school. What was the percent of decrease in the amount of money raised for the school?

(A) 12%
(B) 15%
(C) 18%
(D) 20%
(E) 25%

34. Laundry detergent is sold in 24-cup boxes. If each load needs ⅔ cup of detergent, how many loads will one box of detergent wash?

(A) 8
(B) 12
(C) 36
(D) 72
(E) 108

33. Ⓐ Ⓑ Ⓒ Ⓓ Ⓔ

34. Ⓐ Ⓑ Ⓒ Ⓓ Ⓔ

Answer #33:   (B)

Concept: • Finding a percent of change

Formula: • Percent of change $= \dfrac{\text{Amount of change}}{\text{Original value}}$

Percent of change (both decrease and increase) is always calculated by dividing the amount of the change by the original value. The important thing to keep straight is which value is the "original." In this case, we are determining by what percent the money decreased from last year to this year, so the original value is the amount of money raised last year, or $2,120.

To find the amount of the change, subtract this year's total from last year's total.

$$2,120 - 1,802 = 318$$

The amount of change is 318. Set up your equation.

$$\frac{318}{2,120}$$

Now divide.

$$\frac{318}{2,120} = 0.15, \text{ or } 15\%.$$

Answer #34:   (C)

Concept: • Division with fractions

This problem is asking us, essentially, how many times does $\dfrac{2}{3}$ divide 24. Or, in other words, what is 24 divided by $\dfrac{2}{3}$? Let's set up an equation:

$$\frac{24}{\frac{2}{3}}$$

Now, multiply by the reciprocal of $\dfrac{2}{3}$.

$$24 \cdot \frac{3}{2} = \frac{24 \cdot 3}{2} = 12 \cdot 3 = 36$$

We can get 36 loads of laundry out of one box of detergent.

35. An appliance retailer bought a dishwasher at a wholesale price of $885 and priced it for sale in his store at a retail price of 18% above the wholesale price. During a special sale, he discounted the retail price by 10%. What was the special sale price of the dishwasher?

(A) $1,148.73
(B) $1,044.30
(C) $939.87
(D) $796.50
(E) $700.92

35.

Answer #35: Ⓒ

Concept: • Multiple percent increases or decreases

This problem contains a common trap that catches a lot of people. The trap is in thinking that an increase in price of 18% followed by a discount in price of 10% is equivalent to an increase in 8%. This is the wrong way to think about the problem, because the 10% discount is based on the new price of the item after the 18% increase has been calculated. Let's work through the problem.

The wholesale price is $885, and the retailer adds 18% to that price to get the retail price. Let's multiply 885 by 18% to find the amount of increase.

$$885 \cdot 0.18 = 159.30$$

So we'll add $159.30 to the wholesale price to get the retail price.

$$\$885 + \$159.30 = \$1044.30$$

Now the price is discounted by 10% for a special sale. Let's calculate the 10% discount by multiplying $1044.30 by 10%.

$$1044.30 \cdot 0.10 = 104.43$$

Let's subtract $104.43 from $1044.30 to get the special sale price.

$$\$1044.30 - \$104.43 = \$939.87$$

36. A cat spies a bird sitting at the top of a 20 foot flagpole. If the angle of elevation from the cat to the bird is 36°, how far is the cat from the base of the flagpole?

(A) $20 \tan 36°$

(B) $\dfrac{\tan 36°}{20}$

(C) $\dfrac{\sin 36°}{20}$

(D) $\dfrac{20}{\tan 36°}$

(E) $\dfrac{20}{\sin 36°}$

---

36. Ⓐ Ⓑ Ⓒ Ⓓ Ⓔ

Answer #36: Ⓓ

Concept: • Solving right triangles using trigonometric ratios

Formula: • $\tan \alpha = \dfrac{\text{opposite}}{\text{adjacent}}$

Your first step upon reading this problem should be to draw a sketch so that you can see what the problem is asking. Essentially, the cat, base of the flagpole, and bird form a right triangle.

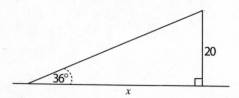

The problem asks for the base of the triangle. Let's make that equal to x. If we know the ratio and have the value of one side of the triangle, we can find the value of x. First, let's figure out if we need to use the sine (opposite over hypotenuse), cosine (adjacent over hypotenuse), or tangent (opposite over adjacent) ratio.

We need to find the tangent of $36°$, since we know the opposite value (20), and are looking for the adjacent value (x). So let's set up a proportion:

$$\frac{\tan 36°}{1} = \frac{20}{x}$$

Now cross-multiply. $\tan 36°(x) = 20$

Divide both sides by $\tan 36°$. $x = \dfrac{20}{\tan 36°}$

37. $(\sqrt{8} + \sqrt{5})(\sqrt{8} - \sqrt{5})$

(A) $\sqrt{39}$

(B) $3\sqrt{13}$

(C) $2\sqrt{19}$

(D) 13

(E) 3

38. A woman bought a house for $396,240. If this figure included the broker's fee of 4% of the price of the house, what was the amount of the broker's fee?

(A) $412,090

(B) $381,000

(C) $16,740

(D) $15,850

(E) $15,240

37. (A) (B) (C) (D) (E)

38. (A) (B) (C) (D) (E)

Answer #37: Ⓔ

Concept: • Quadratic equations
Formula: • $(x + y)(x - y) = x^2 - y^2$

You can solve this problem by using FOIL (First, Outer, Inner, Last).

First: $\sqrt{8} \cdot \sqrt{8} = 8$

Outer: $\sqrt{8} \cdot -\sqrt{5} = -\sqrt{40}$

Inner: $\sqrt{5} \cdot \sqrt{8} = \sqrt{40}$

Last: $\sqrt{5} \cdot -\sqrt{5} = -5$

Now combine: $8 - \sqrt{40} + \sqrt{40} - 5 = 8 - 5 = 3$

Of course, this question is even easier if you know that $(x + y)(x - y) = x^2 + y^2$, since it means that $(\sqrt{8} + \sqrt{5})(\sqrt{8} - \sqrt{5}) = 8 - 5$.

Answer #38: Ⓓ

Concept: • Calculating percents

Before we do any calculations, let's eliminate a few answer choices. The question is asking us for the broker's fee, *not* the price of the house. So answer choices (A) and (B) are way too great. Eliminate them, and we only have three answer choices to deal with.

Now let's calculate the answer to the problem. Do not make the mistake of thinking that we can just calculate 4% of $396,240. That would be the case if the $396,240 was the price of the house *before* the broker's fee was added on. Instead, the $396,240 includes the broker's fee.

The $396,240 amount includes: the price of the house, plus the broker's fee, which is 4% of the price of the house. If we make the price of the house equal to x, then the broker's fee is $0.04x$. Let's put that into an equation:

$396,240 = x + 0.04x$

Combine the variables.

$396,240 = 1.04x$

Divide both sides by 1.04.

$$\frac{381,000}{1.04\overline{)396,240}}$$
$x = 381,000$

So the price of the house is $381,000. Now let's calculate the 4% broker's fee by multiplying 381,000 by 4%.

$381,000 \times 0.04 = 15,240$

The broker's fee is $15,240.

39. In right triangle ABD, if $m\angle B$ = 90° and sin $\angle A = \dfrac{12}{13}$, how long is side $\overline{AB}$?

(A) $\dfrac{5}{12}$

(B) $\dfrac{5}{13}$

(C) 5

(D) 12

(E) 13

40. Line PR intersects line ST at point Q. If the measure of angle PQT is 55°, then what is the measure of angle PQS?

(A) 55°

(B) 65°

(C) 125°

(D) 135°

(E) It cannot be determined from the information given.

39. (A) (B) (C) (D) (E)

40. (A) (B) (C) (D) (E)

Answer #39: Ⓒ

Concepts:
- Solving right triangles using trigonometric ratios
- Evaluating trigonometric functions
- Common side ratios of right triangles

To help answer this question, let's sketch out a triangle and fill in the numbers they give us.

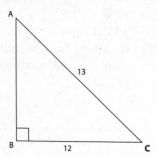

Since sine is $\dfrac{opposite}{hypotenuse}$, 12 is the measure of the side opposite angle A, which is $\overline{BC}$. 13 is the measure of the hypotenuse, which is side $\overline{AC}$.

Now that you know that, you can use the Pythagorean Theorem to calculate the length of side $\overline{AB}$.

$$AB^2 + 12^2 = 13^2$$
$$AB^2 + 144 = 169$$
$$AB^2 = 25$$
$$AB = 5$$

Of course, you could save all those steps if you know that a right triangle with sides 12 and 13 must have another side of 5.

Answer #40: Ⓒ

Concepts:
- Intersecting lines
- Vertical angles
- Supplementary angles

Definition:
- A straight line has 180°.

Let's draw a picture to help solve this problem.

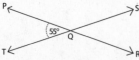

Now that we can see the diagram, it is easy to see that angles PQT and PQS are supplementary angles, which together make a straight line. There are 180° in a straight line, so the measure of angle PQS must be 180° − 55°, or 125°.

41. A certain number is even when it is multiplied by 2, and negative when it is multiplied by 1. The number must be

(A) even
(B) odd
(C) negative
(D) positive
(E) 0

42. A carpenter has a block of wood that is 2 feet high, 4 feet wide, and 5 feet long. The carpenter must cut the wood into 2-inch cubes. How many cubes can the wood be cut into?

(A) 17,280
(B) 8,640
(C) 4,320
(D) 40
(E) 20

41. Ⓐ Ⓑ Ⓒ Ⓓ Ⓔ

42. Ⓐ Ⓑ Ⓒ Ⓓ Ⓔ

Answer #41: (C)

Concept: • Properties of numbers

Definitions: • even × even = even
• even × odd = even
• positive × positive = postive
• positive × negative = negative

The best way to work this problem is to go step-by-step to eliminate the answer choices. If the number is even when it is multiplied by 2, it could be either even or odd. For instance, 2 × 2 = 4, but 3 × 2 = 6. That means the number could be either even or odd. Eliminate answer choices (A) and (B).

If the number is negative when it is multiplied by 1, the number itself must be negative. Since any number multiplied by 1 stays the same, a positive number multiplied by 1 cannot be negative. The answer is (C). Eliminate (D).

(E) cannot be the answer, because 0 times 1 is 0, which is not negative.

Answer #42: (B)

Concepts: • Volume of a rectangular solid
• Volume of a cube
• Conversion of units

Formulas: • Volume of a rectangular solid = lwh
• Volume of a cube = s^3
• 12 inches = 1 foot

Since the problem gives us information about feet and asks us for an answer in inches, let's do our conversion now. If the block of wood is 2 feet by 4 feet by 5 feet, it is 24 inches by 48 inches by 60 inches.

If each cube has a side of 2 inches, then we can get 12 cubes from the 24-inch height of the block, 24 cubes from the 48-inch width of the block, and 30 cubes from the 60-inch length of the block.

$$12 \times 24 \times 30 = 8,640$$

We can cut 8,640 2-inch cubes from the block of wood.

43. If the area of an equilateral triangle is $16\sqrt{3}$, what is the length of a side of the triangle?

(A) 4
(B) $4\sqrt{3}$
(C) 8
(D) $8\sqrt{3}$
(E) 16

44. If the slope of a line is $-\dfrac{3}{2}$ and one point on the line is $(0,2)$, then if another point on the line is $(x, 8)$, what is the value of x?

(A) -8
(B) -4
(C) 0
(D) 2
(E) 4

---

43. Ⓐ Ⓑ Ⓒ Ⓓ Ⓔ

44. Ⓐ Ⓑ Ⓒ Ⓓ Ⓔ

Answer #43: Ⓒ

Concepts:
- Area of a triangle
- Side length ratios for 30-60-90 triangles

Formula:
- Area of a triangle is $\frac{1}{2}bh$
- The sides of a 30-60-90 triangle are x, $2x$, and $x\sqrt{3}$

To find the area of a triangle we need to know the base and the height. The height of an equilateral triangle is found by dropping a line from the top vertex at a right angle to the base. This creates two 30-60-90 triangles.

Each one of these 30-60-90 triangles has the same height, but only half the base, of the equilateral triangle. The ratio of the sides of a 30-60-90 triangle also tells you what the lengths of these sides must be. The base must be x and the height must be $x\sqrt{3}$. (The third side is $2x$.) Since the base times the height of the 30-60-90 triangle is $16\sqrt{3}$, which is $x^2\sqrt{3}$, x must be 4.

This means the sides of the 30-60-90 triangle are 4, $4\sqrt{3}$, and 8. The length of a side of the equilateral triangle is 8.

Answer #44: Ⓑ

Concept:
- Equation of a line

Definitions:
- Slope
- y-intercept

Formula:
- $y = mx + b$

This question is asking us to write the equation of a line using the numbers it gives. In the line equation, $y = mx + b$, x and y are coordinates, m is the slope, and b is the y-intercept. The slope is $-\frac{3}{2}$, and the y-intercept is 2, so the equation is

$$y = -\frac{3}{2}x + 2$$

Now we can put the point $(x, 8)$ into the equation and solve for x.

$$8 = -\frac{3}{2}x + 2$$

Subtract 2 from both sides.

$$6 = -\frac{3}{2}x$$

Multiply both sides by 2.

$$12 = -3x$$

Divide both sides by -3.

$$-4 = x$$

45. If an alloy contains 6 parts silver, 2 parts gold, and 1 part aluminum by weight, how many ounces of gold are in 459 ounces of the alloy?

(A) 51
(B) 102
(C) 306
(D) 457
(E) 918

46. The endpoints of line *CD* are $(-1, 5)$ and $(5, -3)$. If line *FG* bisects line *CD*, at what point does line *FG* intersect with line *CD*?

(A) $(-1, -3)$
(B) $(2, 1)$
(C) $(2, 5)$
(D) $(5, 1)$
(E) $(5, 5)$

---

45. (A) (B) (C) (D) (E)

46. (A) (B) (C) (D) (E)

Answer #45: (B)

Concept: • Ratios

6 parts silver to 2 parts gold to 1 part aluminum tells us the ratio of the ingredients of the alloy. This ratio holds true no matter how much or how little of the alloy we have. $6 + 2 + 1 = 9$, so we should think in terms of 9 total parts in the ratio.

If there are 459 ounces of the alloy, and there are 9 parts of the ratio, then we can divide 459 by 9 to figure out how many times the steady ratio of the ingredients goes into the actual amount.

$$\frac{51}{9)459}$$

This means that there are 6×51, or 306, ounces of silver in the 459 ounces of alloy, 2×51, or 102, ounces of gold in the 459 ounces of alloy, and 1×51, or 51, ounces of aluminum in the 459 ounces of alloy.

The question asks for the amount of gold, so the correct answer is (B).

Answer #46: (B)

Concept: • The midpoint formula
Definition: • Bisect
Formula: • Midpoint $= \left(\dfrac{x_1 + x_2}{2}, \dfrac{y_1 + y_2}{2}\right)$

"Bisect" means to cut something exactly in half. So line *FG* will intersect line *CD* at the midpoint of line *CD*.

To find the midpoint, let's use the midpoint formula.

$$\left(\frac{-1 + 5}{2}, \frac{5 - 3}{2}\right) = \left(\frac{4}{2}, \frac{2}{2}\right) = (2, 1)$$

If the answer choices are very far apart (as they are in this problem), you could always sketch the problem out as a last resort. Graph the line and mark the midpoint, then guesstimate the coordinates of that point and choose the closest answer from the answer choices. Obviously, however, it's safest to use the midpoint formula.

47. In triangle ABC, $\overline{AB}$ is perpendicular to $\overline{BC}$. If m$\angle B = 3x$ and m$\angle C = 2x - 20$, then what is the measure of angle A?

   (A) 30°
   (B) 40°
   (C) 50°
   (D) 60°
   (E) 80°

48. The value-sized bottle of lotion contains 40% more lotion than the regular-sized bottle does. If the value-sized bottle contains 56 ounces of lotion, how much lotion does the regular-sized bottle contain?

   (A) 40
   (B) 42
   (C) 48
   (D) 52
   (E) 72

---

47. Ⓐ   Ⓑ   Ⓒ   Ⓓ   Ⓔ

48. Ⓐ   Ⓑ   Ⓒ   Ⓓ   Ⓔ

Answer #47: Ⓒ

Concepts:	• Degrees in a triangle
	• Right triangles
Definition:	• A triangle has 180°

If $\overline{AB}$ is perpendicular to $\overline{BC}$, they meet at a right angle. This means that the measure of angle B is 90°. Since $3x = 90°$, $x = 30°$.

Put 30 in for x to find the measure of angle C.

$$2(30) - 20 = 60 - 20 = 40$$

The measure of angle C is 40°. Since there are 180° in a triangle, and the measures of angles B and C are 90° and 40° respectively, the measure of angle A must be 180° − (90° + 40°) = 180° − 130°, or 50°.

Answer #48: Ⓐ

Concept:	• Finding the original value before a percent increase
Formula:	• Percent change $= \dfrac{\text{amount of change}}{\text{original value}}$

Let's make $x =$ the amount of lotion in a regular-sized bottle. Since the value-sized bottle contains 40% more than the regular-sized bottle, it contains $0.4x$ more than x.

$$x + 0.4x = 1.4x$$

The value-sized bottle contains $1.4x$, which the problem tells us is equal to 56 ounces.

$$1.4x = 56$$

Divide both sides by 1.4.

$$x = 40$$

So there are 40 ounces in a regular-sized bottle of lotion.

49. In triangle ABC, m$\angle A$ is 3 times m$\angle B$, and m$\angle C$ is twice m$\angle A$. How many degrees are in angle A?

(A) 18
(B) 36
(C) 48
(D) 54
(E) 108

50. If xy is a positive, odd integer, then which of the following cannot be the value of y?

(A) -121
(B) -1
(C) $\dfrac{1}{3}$
(D) 1
(E) 4

49. Ⓐ Ⓑ Ⓒ Ⓓ Ⓔ

50. Ⓐ Ⓑ Ⓒ Ⓓ Ⓔ

Answer #49: Ⓓ

Concepts: • Ratios
• 180° in a triangle

Let's rewrite the information from the problem to make the ratios of the angles more clear:

The ratio of $\angle C : \angle A : \angle B$ is 6:3:1.

Since there are 180° in a triangle, we can use this ratio to set up an equation.

$6x + 3x + x = 180$

Combine the variables.

$10x = 180$

Divide both sides by 10.

$x = 18$

This means that m$\angle B$ is 18°. Careful, though—the problem asks about m$\angle A$. The ratio of m$\angle A$: m$\angle B$ is 3:1. Let's multiply 18 by 3 to get the measure of $\angle A$.

$3 \times 18 = 54$

m$\angle A$ is 54°.

Answer #50: Ⓔ

Let's take the information from the problem one step at a time.

Since xy is positive, either both x and y must be positive, or both x and y must be negative. For example, if $x = 5$ and $y = 3$, then $xy = 15$. Also, if $x = -5$ and $y = -3$, then $xy = 15$.

Since xy is odd, both x and y must be odd. This is because any number multiplied by an even number becomes even.

Since xy is an integer, either x or y could be a fraction, as long as xy remains a positive, odd integer. For example, if $y = \frac{1}{3}$ and $x = 9$, then $xy = \frac{1}{3} \times 9$, or 3.

Knowing all this, we can eliminate answer choices (A) and (B), because they are negative (which is OK) and odd (which is also OK).

We can eliminate answer choice (C), because we've shown that a fraction can be OK.

We can eliminate answer choice (D), because it is positive (which is OK) and odd (which is also OK).

Answer choice (E) is the answer, because if y is 4, then xy will have to be even.

51. How many minutes are there in x hours, y minutes, and z seconds?

(A) $60x + y + \dfrac{60}{z}$

(B) $x + 60y + 60z$

(C) $\dfrac{x}{60} + y + \dfrac{60}{z}$

(D) $60x + 60y + z$

(E) $60x + y + \dfrac{z}{60}$

52. If k bricks weigh p pounds, then how many pounds do r bricks weigh?

(A) $\dfrac{pk}{r}$

(B) $\dfrac{k}{pr}$

(C) $\dfrac{pr}{k}$

(D) $\dfrac{kr}{p}$

(E) $\dfrac{p}{kr}$

51. Ⓐ Ⓑ Ⓒ Ⓓ Ⓔ

52. Ⓐ Ⓑ Ⓒ Ⓓ Ⓔ

Answer #51: Ⓔ

Concept: • Conversion of units of time

Let's work this problem one step at a time.

There are 60 minutes per hour, so there are $60x$ minutes in x hours. In y minutes there are y minutes.

Each second is $\frac{1}{60}$ of a minute, so there are $\frac{z}{60}$ minutes in z seconds.

Add these all together, to get $60x + y + \frac{z}{60}$.

If you are still confused, you can check your answer by putting in some real numbers to try it out. For example, let's try 2 hours, 10 minutes, and 120 seconds. This is a total of 120 minutes (for 2 hours) + 10 minutes + 2 minutes (for 120 seconds), or 132 minutes. Putting this into the equation $60x + y + \frac{z}{60}$, we get $60(2) + 10 + \frac{120}{60} = 120 + 10 + 2 = 132$. Answer choice (E) works.

Answer #52: Ⓒ

Concept: • Solving proportions
            • Solving problems with several unknowns

Formula: • If $\frac{a}{d} = \frac{b}{c}$ then $ac = bd$

To solve this problem, let's set up a proportion. First, let's make $x =$ the number of pounds r bricks weigh. Then, we'll set up a proportion so that we can compare bricks to bricks and pounds to pounds.

$$\frac{\text{bricks}}{\text{pounds}} = \frac{\text{bricks}}{\text{pounds}}, \text{ or } \frac{k}{p} = \frac{r}{x}$$

Now let's solve for x. Cross-multiply.

$$kx = pr$$

Divide both sides by k.

$$x = \frac{pr}{k}$$

So $\frac{pr}{k}$ is the answer.

53. Caitlin spent $\frac{1}{4}$ of her paycheck on books, and $\frac{2}{3}$ of what was left on clothes. If she didn't buy anything else, and had $40 left, how much money was in her paycheck?

(A) $160
(B) $180
(C) $195
(D) $200
(E) $240

53. Ⓐ Ⓑ Ⓒ Ⓓ Ⓔ

Answer #53: (A)

Concept: • Solving word problems

Let's work this problem a step at a time.

If Caitlin spent $\frac{1}{4}$ of her paycheck on books, then she had $\frac{3}{4}$ of it left. Then she spent $\frac{2}{3}$ of what was left. Let's multiply $\frac{2}{3}$ by the $\frac{3}{4}$ that's left.

$$\frac{2}{3} \times \frac{3}{4} = \frac{6}{12} = \frac{1}{2}$$

So she spent $\frac{1}{2}$ of her original paycheck on clothes. She spent $\frac{1}{4}$ and then $\frac{1}{2}$, so she spent a total of $\frac{1}{4} + \frac{1}{2}$, or $\frac{3}{4}$, of her total paycheck. Therefore, she has $\frac{1}{4}$ of the paycheck left.

If she has $40 left, then $40 is equal to $\frac{1}{4}$ of her paycheck. To figure out what the entire paycheck was, let's set up a proportion. We'll make $x =$ the total paycheck.

$$\frac{1}{4} = \frac{40}{x}$$

Cross-multiply.

$$x = 160$$

So the total paycheck was $160.

54. If $x = -2$, then
$$\frac{(4 + x)(x - 3) + 5}{x + 10} =$$

(A) $-\dfrac{3}{2}$

(B) $-\dfrac{5}{8}$

(C) $-\dfrac{1}{12}$

(D) $\dfrac{5}{8}$

(E) $\dfrac{3}{2}$

54. Ⓐ Ⓑ Ⓒ Ⓓ Ⓔ

Answer #54: Ⓑ

Concept: • Order of operations

To solve this problem, remember the order of operations. You probably learned PEMDAS (sometimes remembered as Please Excuse My Dear Aunt Sally) as a way to keep the order of operations clear. PEMDAS stands for

Parentheses
Exponents
Multiplication
Division
Addition
Subtraction

Let's put in -2 whenever we see x, then solve the equation using the order of operations.

$$\frac{(4 + -2)(-2 - 3) + 5}{-2 + 10}$$

Solve within the parentheses.

$$\frac{(2)(-5) + 5}{8}$$

Now multiply.

$$\frac{-10 + 5}{8}$$

Solve the fraction.

$$-\frac{5}{8}$$

55. If $6x - 5y = 25$ and $3y - x = 12$, then what is the value of $5x - 2y$?

(A) 0
(B) 13
(C) 24
(D) 37
(E) 50

56. If $6k - 4p^2 = 2$ and $\sqrt{6k} + 2p = 1$, then what is the value of $\sqrt{6k} - 2p$?

(A) -2
(B) -1
(C) 0
(D) $\dfrac{1}{2}$
(E) 2

---

55. (A) (B) (C) (D) (E)

56. (A) (B) (C) (D) (E)

Answer #55: Ⓓ

Concept: • Simultaneous equations

Although this problem may look tough, it's really just a matter of untangling the simultaneous equations. First, let's write out the complete equations we're given.

$$6x - 5y = 25$$
$$3y - x = 12$$

Can we add those together to get anything that looks like the expression $5x - 2y$? No. Let's rearrange.

$$6x - 5y = 25$$
$$-x + 3y = 12$$

Now we're making progress. If we add the second equation to the first equation, we'll end up with the expression $5x - 2y$. Let's do it.

$$\begin{array}{r} 6x - 5y = 25 \\ -x + 3y = 12 \\ \hline 5x - 2y = 37 \end{array}$$

So $5x - 2y = 37$.

Answer #56: Ⓔ

Concept: • Factoring the difference of two squares

Formula: • $x^2 - y^2 = (x + y)(x - y)$

At first glance, this problem is a killer. However, upon closer inspection it reveals itself to be a trickier way of writing

$$6k - 4p^2 = (\sqrt{6k} + 2p)(\sqrt{6k} - 2p)$$

You can factor this out the long way, but you will be much happier if you memorize the expression $x^2 - y^2 = (x + y)(x - y)$ and use it on the test!

Since $6k - 4p^2 = 2$ and $\sqrt{6k} + 2p = 1$, we can rewrite the equation.

$$2 = (1)(x), \text{ where } x \text{ is the value of } \sqrt{6k} - 2p.$$

Divide both sides by 1.

$$2 = x$$

So $\sqrt{6k} - 2p = 2$.

57. At a buffet dinner for 60 guests, 28 guests had the fish, 34 guests had the chicken, and 8 guests had neither the fish nor the chicken. How many guests had both the fish and the chicken?

(A) 8
(B) 10
(C) 12
(D) 14
(E) 20

58. At a certain company, 82% of the employees drive their cars to work. If 738 employees do not drive their cars to work, how many employees work for the company?

(A) 820
(B) 900
(C) 3,600
(D) 4,100
(E) 4,240

57. Ⓐ Ⓑ Ⓒ Ⓓ Ⓔ

58. Ⓐ Ⓑ Ⓒ Ⓓ Ⓔ

Answer #57: Ⓑ

Concept:
- Solving word problems involving groups
- Alternatives to the Venn Diagram

This problem is exactly the kind of problem you've been taught to draw a Venn Diagram to solve. However, it is just as easy to solve this problem without the interlocking circles.

The trick is setting up your equation correctly. Essentially, we have 5 elements in the question: the "total" of all the people, "fish" people, "chicken" people, "both" people, and "neither" people.

To put them into an equation, we're going to add the groups that don't overlap: fish, chicken, and neither. Then we'll make them equal to the total. But, and this is the key to the whole thing, we have to subtract the "both" people so we don't end up counting them twice.

The equation ends up looking like this:

Fish + Chicken + Neither − Both = Total

Now, stick in the numbers and solve. Make b = Both.

$$28 + 34 + 8 - b = 60$$

Combine. $70 - b = 60$

Add b to both sides. $70 = 60 + b$

Subtract 60 from both sides. $10 = b$

So 10 guests had both fish and chicken.

Answer #58 Ⓓ

Concept:
- Solving percent problems
- Using proportions

Since 82% drive their cars to work, then 18% do not drive their cars to work. 738 is the number of employees who do not drive their cars to work, so 738 represents 18% of the company. To figure out how many employees there are in the entire company, we can set up a proportion. Let's make x = the total employees. Since percent means "per one hundred," we'll put 18 over 100 to represent 18%.

$$\frac{18}{100} = \frac{738}{x}$$

Cross-multiply. $18x = 73,800$

Divide both sides by 18. $x = 4,100$

59. If $\dfrac{\sqrt{x}+k}{y-\sqrt{x}} = 18$ and

$\dfrac{y-\sqrt{x}}{k-\sqrt{x}} = 4$, then what is

the value of $\dfrac{k-\sqrt{x}}{\sqrt{x}+k}$?

(A) 72

(B) 22

(C) $\dfrac{9}{2}$

(D) $\dfrac{2}{9}$

(E) $\dfrac{1}{72}$

59. Ⓐ Ⓑ Ⓒ Ⓓ Ⓔ

Answer #59: Ⓔ

Concept: • Algebraic manipulation of fractions
Definition: • Reciprocal

This question can kill you if you attempt to solve for k, x, and y. There's no way to do it. Notice, however, that the question doesn't actually ask you for the individual values of k, x, and y, but for the value of a fraction containing those variables. It is possible to find the answer to the question by rearranging the fractions.

Let's try multiplying them.

$$\frac{\sqrt{x} + k}{y - \sqrt{x}} \times \frac{y - \sqrt{x}}{k - \sqrt{x}} = \frac{(\sqrt{x} + k)(y - \sqrt{x})}{(y - \sqrt{x})(k - \sqrt{x})}$$

We can divide the $y - \sqrt{x}$ in the numerator and denominator. This leaves us with the fraction

$$\frac{\sqrt{x} + k}{k - \sqrt{x}}$$

Since we multiplied the two equations, we can multiply their values, too.

$$18 \times 4 = 72$$

This means that $\dfrac{\sqrt{x} + k}{k - \sqrt{x}} = 72$.

Unfortunately, the question asks us for the value of $\dfrac{k - \sqrt{x}}{\sqrt{x} + k}$, not $\dfrac{\sqrt{x} + k}{k - \sqrt{x}}$. That's not a problem, though, because if $\dfrac{\sqrt{x} + k}{k - \sqrt{x}} = 72$, then it also means that $\dfrac{\sqrt{x} + k}{k - \sqrt{x}} = \dfrac{72}{1}$. We can take the reciprocal of the fraction, and we can do the same thing with the answer.

$$\frac{k - \sqrt{x}}{\sqrt{x} + k} = \frac{1}{72}$$

60. A square is inscribed in a
circle. If the area of the
square is 100, what is the
area of the circle?

(A) $10\sqrt{2}\pi$

(B) $25\sqrt{2}\pi$

(C) 50π

(D) $50\sqrt{2}\pi$

(E) 100π

60. Ⓐ Ⓑ Ⓒ Ⓓ Ⓔ

Answer #60: $\copyright$

Concepts: • Area of a square
   • Area of a circle

Formulas: • Area of a circle $= \pi r^2$
   • Area of a square $= s^2$

Let's draw a picture to help visualize this problem.

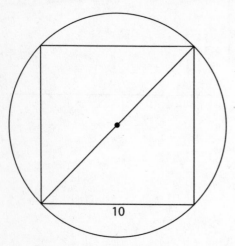

Since the area of the square is 100, each side must be 10. That means that the diagonal is $10\sqrt{2}$. We can use the Pythagorean Theorem to calculate that, but it's much more direct to have memorized the side relationships of the 45-45-90 triangle (half of a square), which are a, a, and $a\sqrt{2}$.

The diagonal of the square is the diameter of the circle. Since the diameter of the circle is $10\sqrt{2}$, the radius is half that, or $5\sqrt{2}$. To find the area of the circle, we should use the formula πr^2.

$$5\sqrt{2} \times 5\sqrt{2} \times \pi = 25 \times 2 \times \pi = 50\,\pi.$$

So the area of the circle is 50π.

CONCEPT-TO-PROBLEM INDEX

Each problem on the SAT tests one or more math concepts. This index lists the 120 problems in this book by the concepts each tests. As you are working the two SAT tests, circle in this index the problem numbers that you get wrong or have difficulty with. When you are done with the tests, you can then look at this index and clearly identify those skills that you need to practice. Conversely, you can use this index to get directly to those types of problems you now you need help with. Those concepts in the tests that come under the "other" category are written with a star (☆) following them. For example, problem 6 on page 23 tests the concept of repeating sequences. (Note: The numbers listed for each concept refer to the test number, problem number, and page number. For example, 1–25(43) refers to test 1, problem 25, which appears on page 43.)

Algebra

Averages............... 1–22(39), 1–36(57), 1–49(73), 1–57(81)

Functions .... 1–15(33), 1–34(55)

Probability .... 1–21(39), 1–55(79)

Rates .... 1–5(27), 1–10(27), 1–12(29), 1–16(33), 1–17(35), 1–42(651), 1–60(83)

Solving equations .... 1–41(65), 2–4(89), 2–9(95), 2–12(97), 2–16(103), 2–19(107), 2–23(115), 2–26(119), 2–55(153)

Word problems .... 1–3(21), 1–9(27), 1–15(33), 1–24(41), 2–8(93)

Arithmetic

Arithmetic . . . . 1-7(25), 1-8(25), 1-15(33), 1-25(43), 1-28(49), 1-31(57), 1-44(67), 1-51(75), 2-1(87), 2-8(93), 2-14(99), 2-24(115), 2-45(141), 2-48(143), 2-51(147), 2-53(149)

Exponents and square
roots . . . . 1-20(37), 1-25(43), 1-27(47), 1-32(53), 1-44(67), 1-47(71), 1-52(75), 1-59(83), 2-5(91), 2-6(91), 2-37(133)

Factoring and prime   1-1(19), 1-8(25), 1-26(47), 1-59(83), 2-11(97),
factors . . . . 2-18(105), 2-27(121), 2-42(137)

Fractions . . . . 1-16(33), 1-29(49), 1-47(71), 1-55(79), 2-11(97), 2-18(105), 2-27(121), 2-42(137)

Inequalities . . . . 1-20(37), 1-39(59)

Percentages . . . . 1-9(27), 1-35(55), 1-46(69), 2-2(87), 2-3(89), 2-13(99), 2-18(105), 2-20(109), 2-24(115), 2-29(123}, 2-31(125), 2-33(127), 2-35(129), 2-38(133), 2-58(155)

Polynomial
arithmetic . . . . 1-4(21), 1-11(29), 1-14(31)

Ratios . . . . 2-10(95), 2-32(125), 2-49(145), 2-52(147)

Geometry

Circle geometry . . . . 1-23(41), 1-40(61)

Coordinate geometry . . . . 1-18(35), 1-37(57), 1-45(69), 1-56(79), 2-7(93), 2-25(117), 2-44(139), 2-46(141)

Rectangle geometry . . . . . 1-13(31), 1-23(41), 1-48(71), 1-50(73), 2-15(101), 2-20(109), 2-28(121)

Triangle geometry . . . . 1-2(19), 1-19(37), 1-33(53), 1-38(59), 1-43(67), 1-50(73), 1-54(77), 1-58(81), 2-17(105), 2-43(139), 2-47(143), 2-49(145), 2-60(159)

Other

Diagramming .... 1-48(71), 1-50(73),
                        1-54(77), 1-58(81)

Tables and graphs .... 1-46(69), 1-53(77)

Trigonometry .... 2-22(113), 2-30(123),
                        2-36(131), 2-39(135)

Other☆ .... 1-6(23), 1-7(25),
                        1-12(29), 1-16(33),
                        1-28(49), 1-30(51),
                        2-57(155)

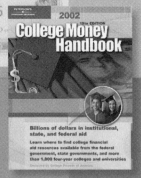